DUSK'S EMBRACE THE CITY'S QUIET HEART

COLORING BOOK

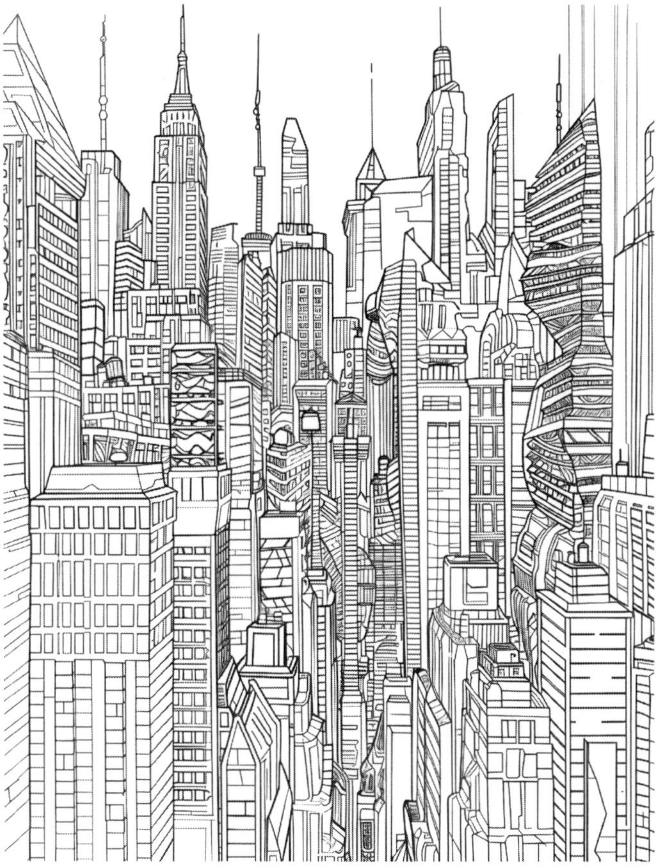

This book belongs to

....

TEST YOUR COLORS HERE

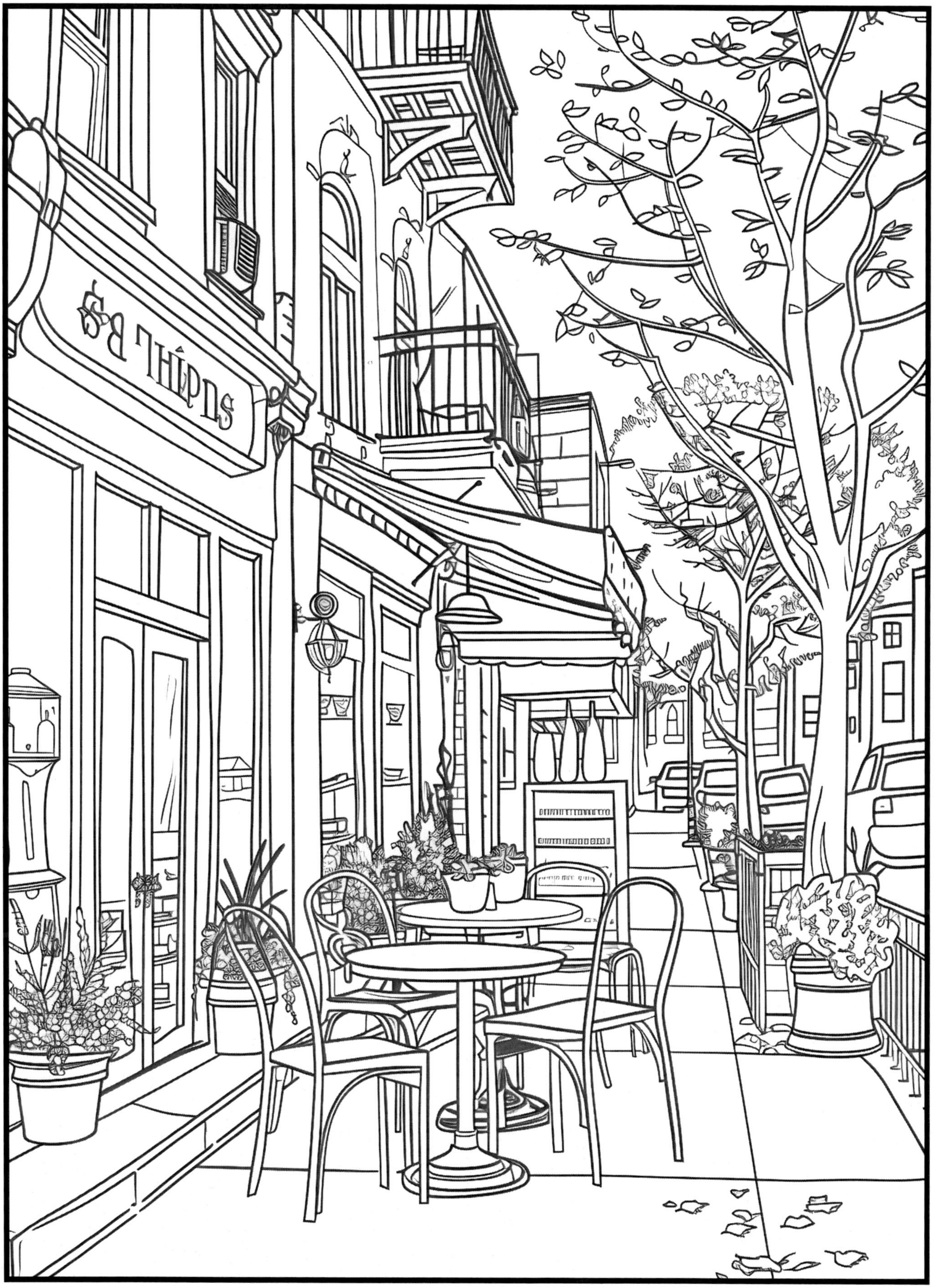

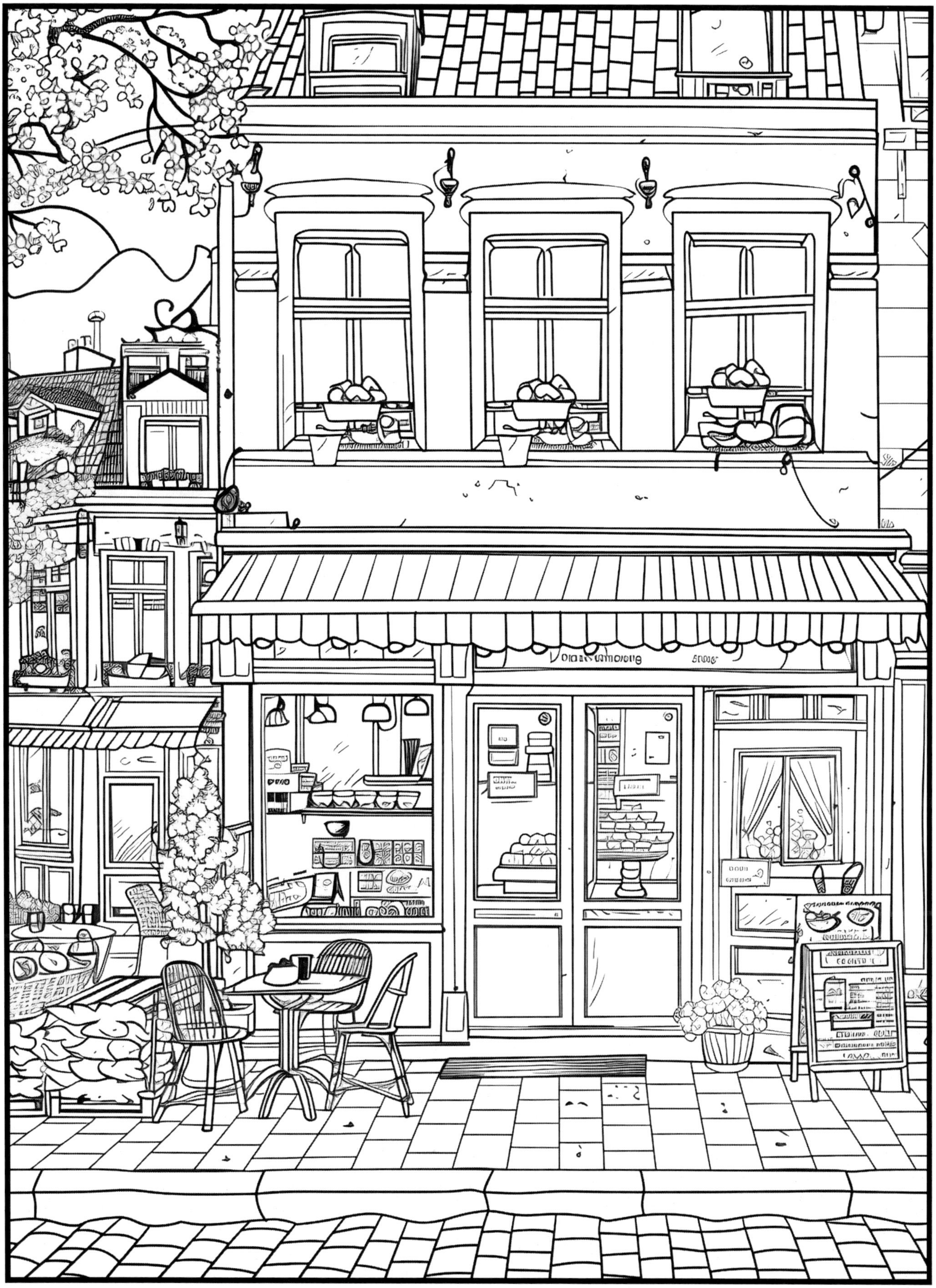

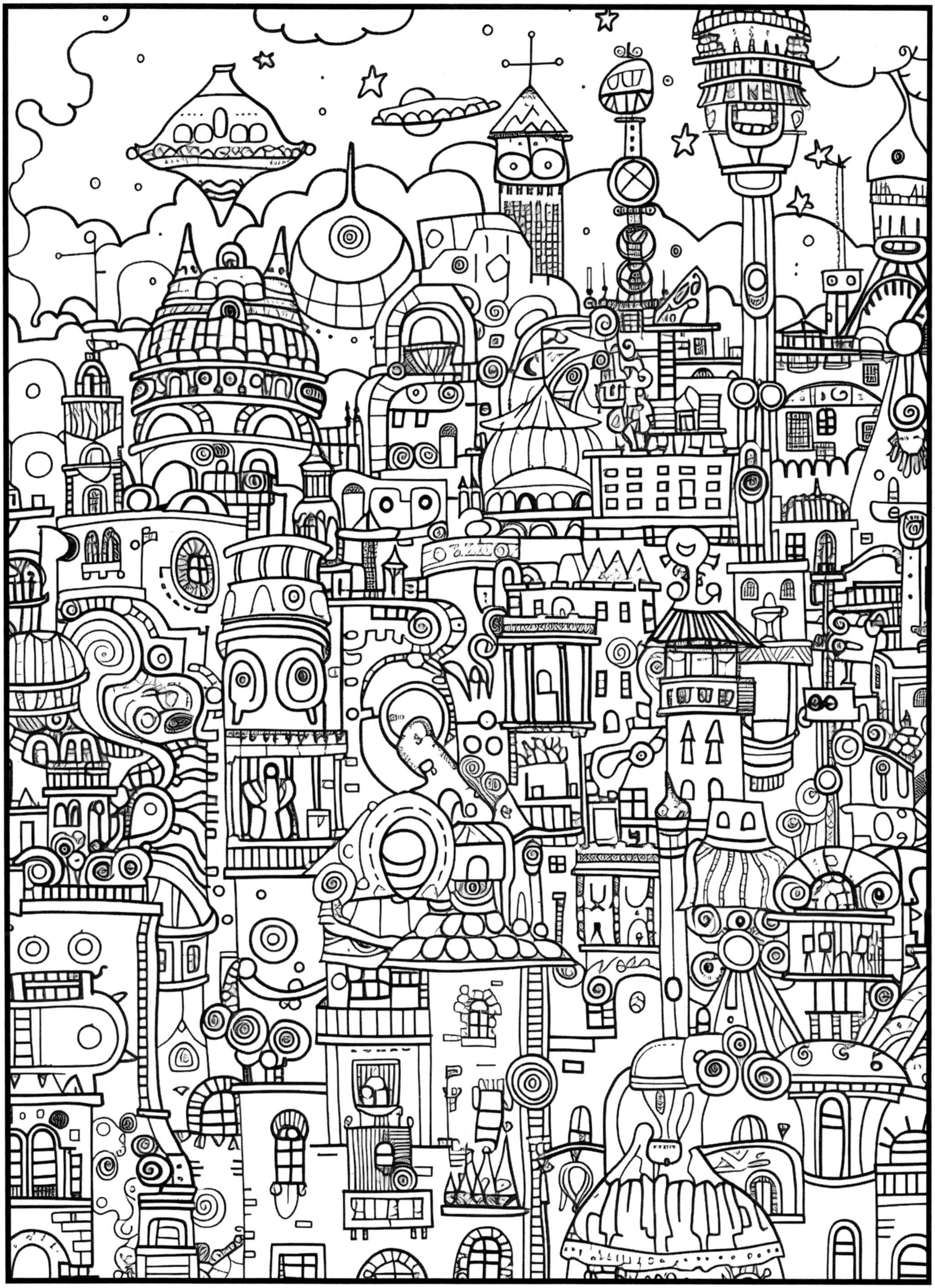

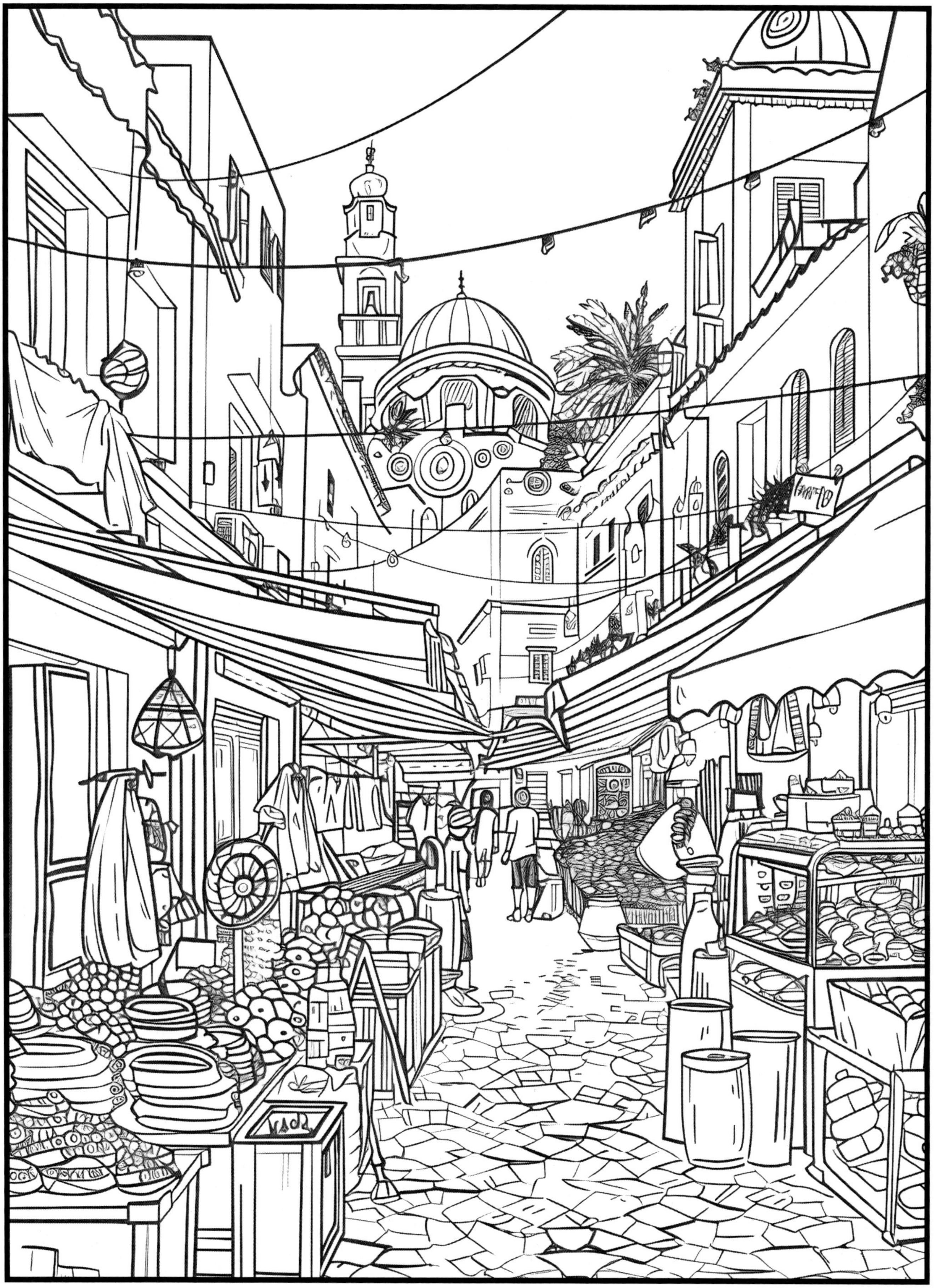

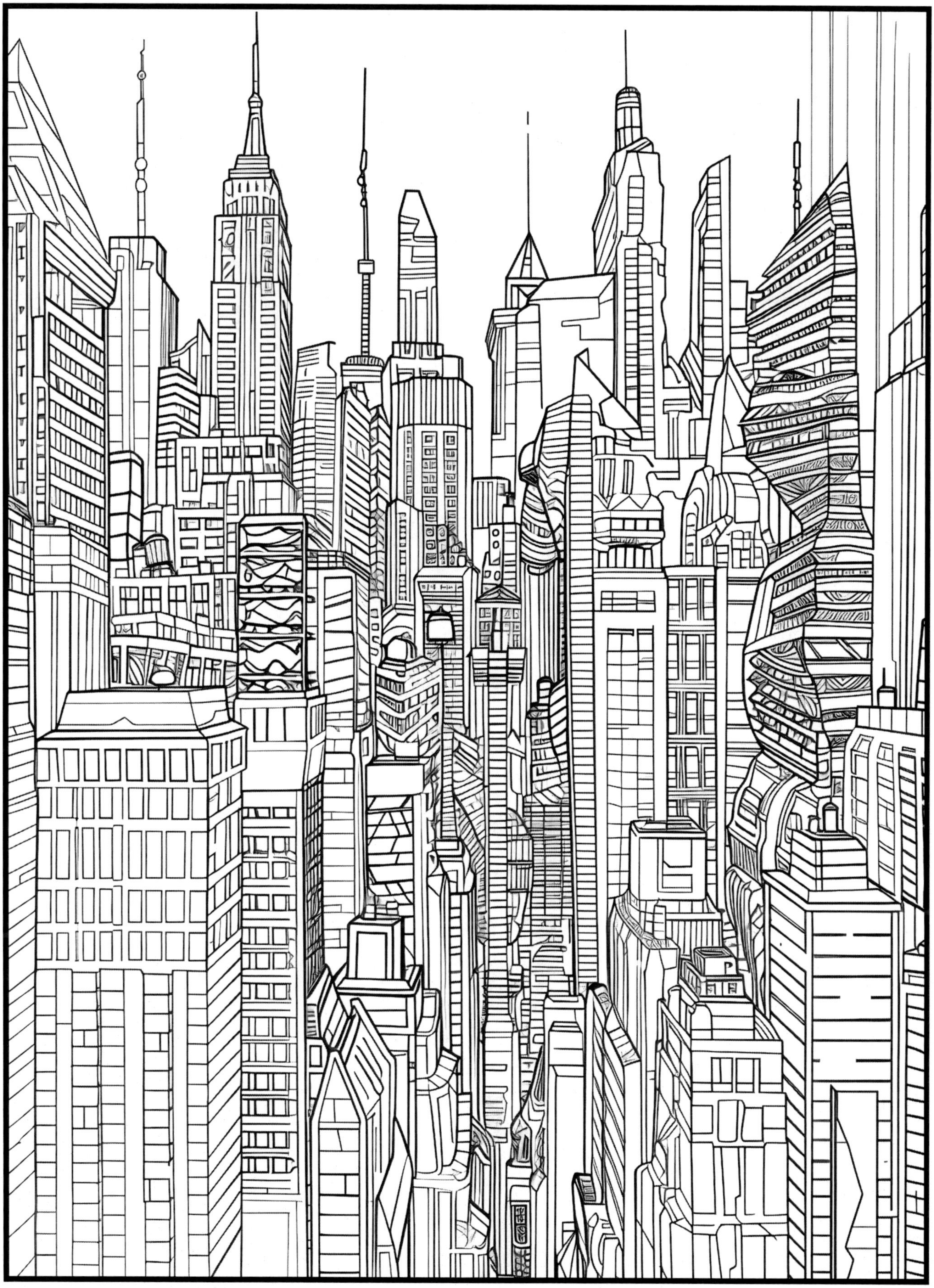

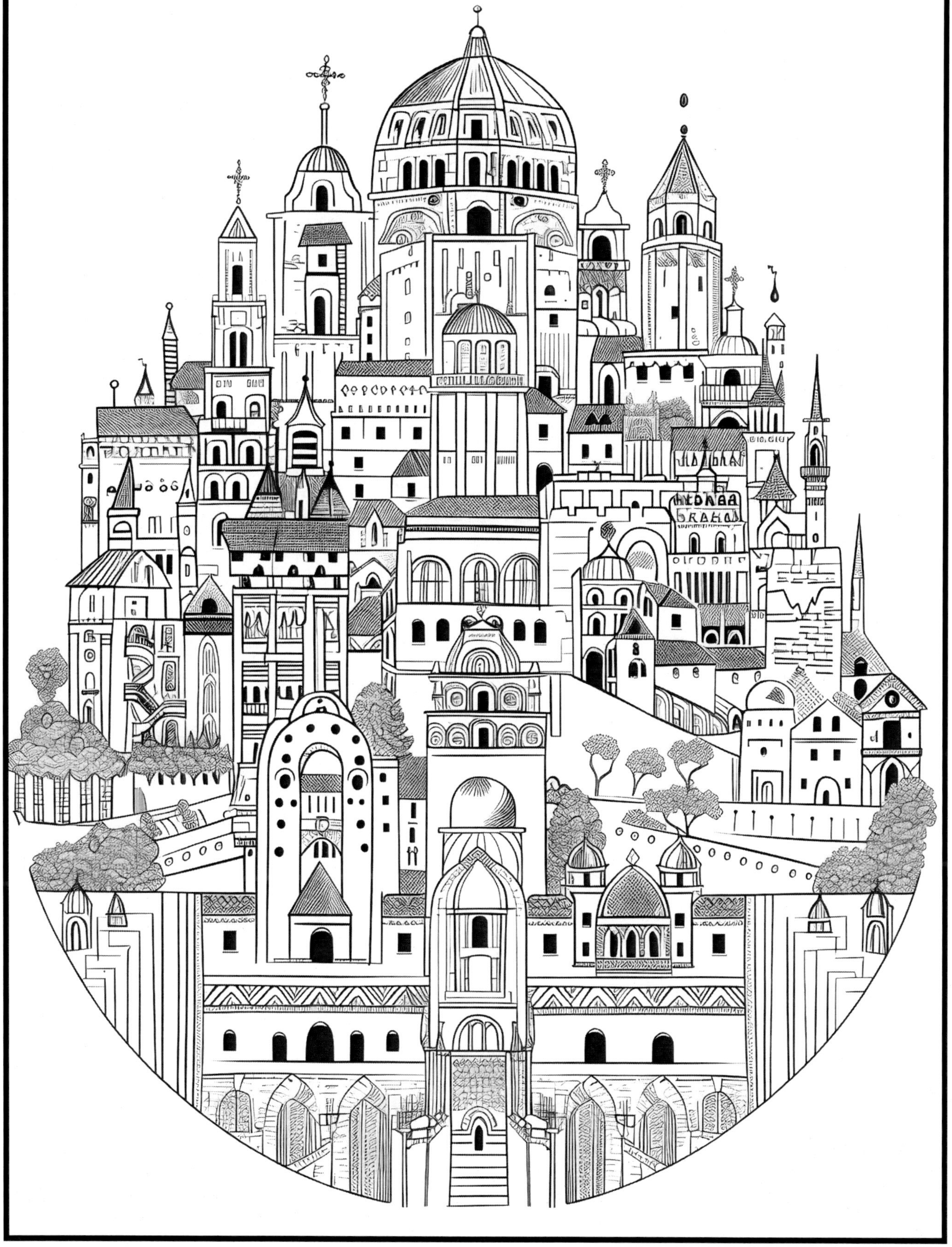

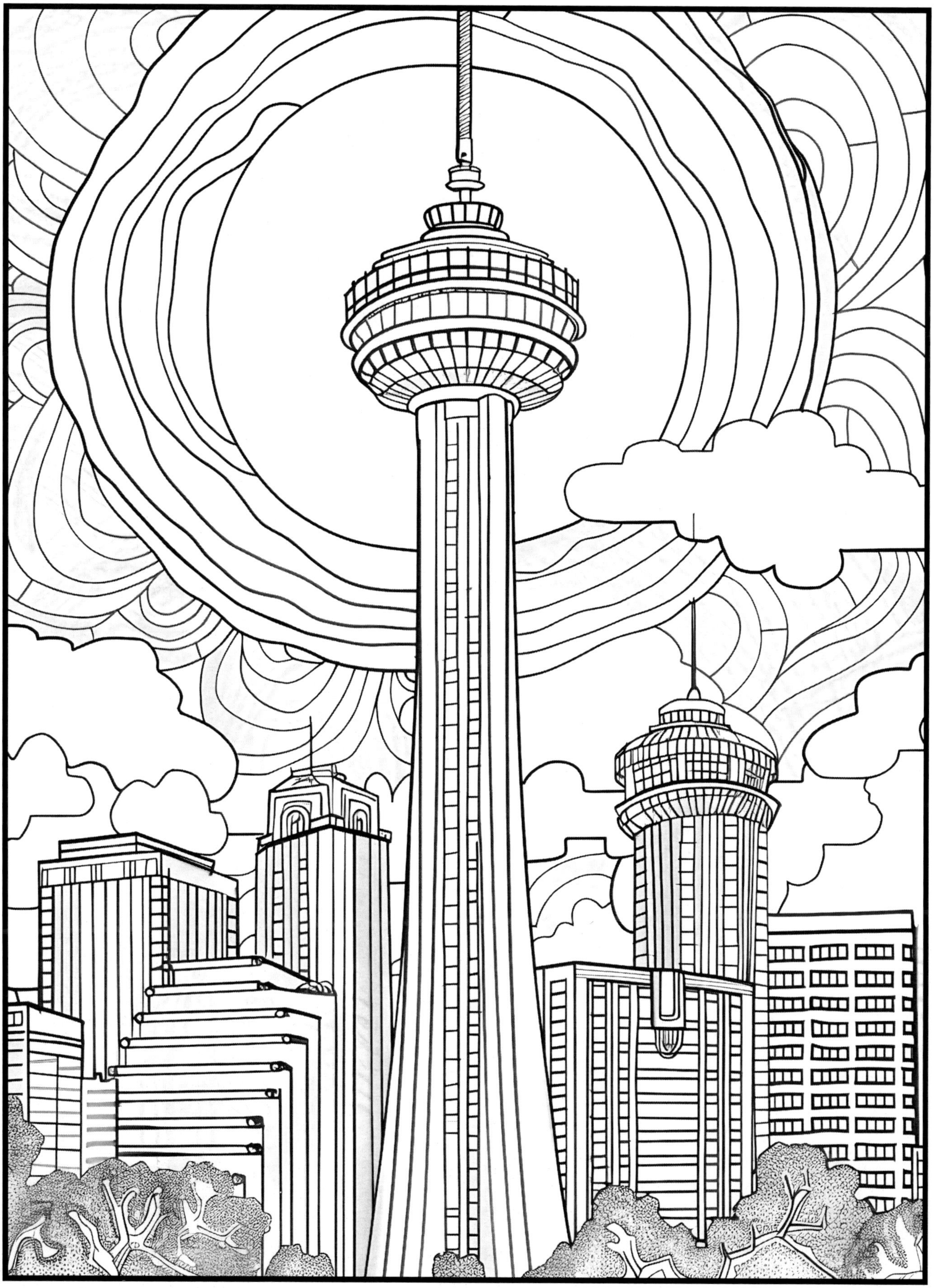

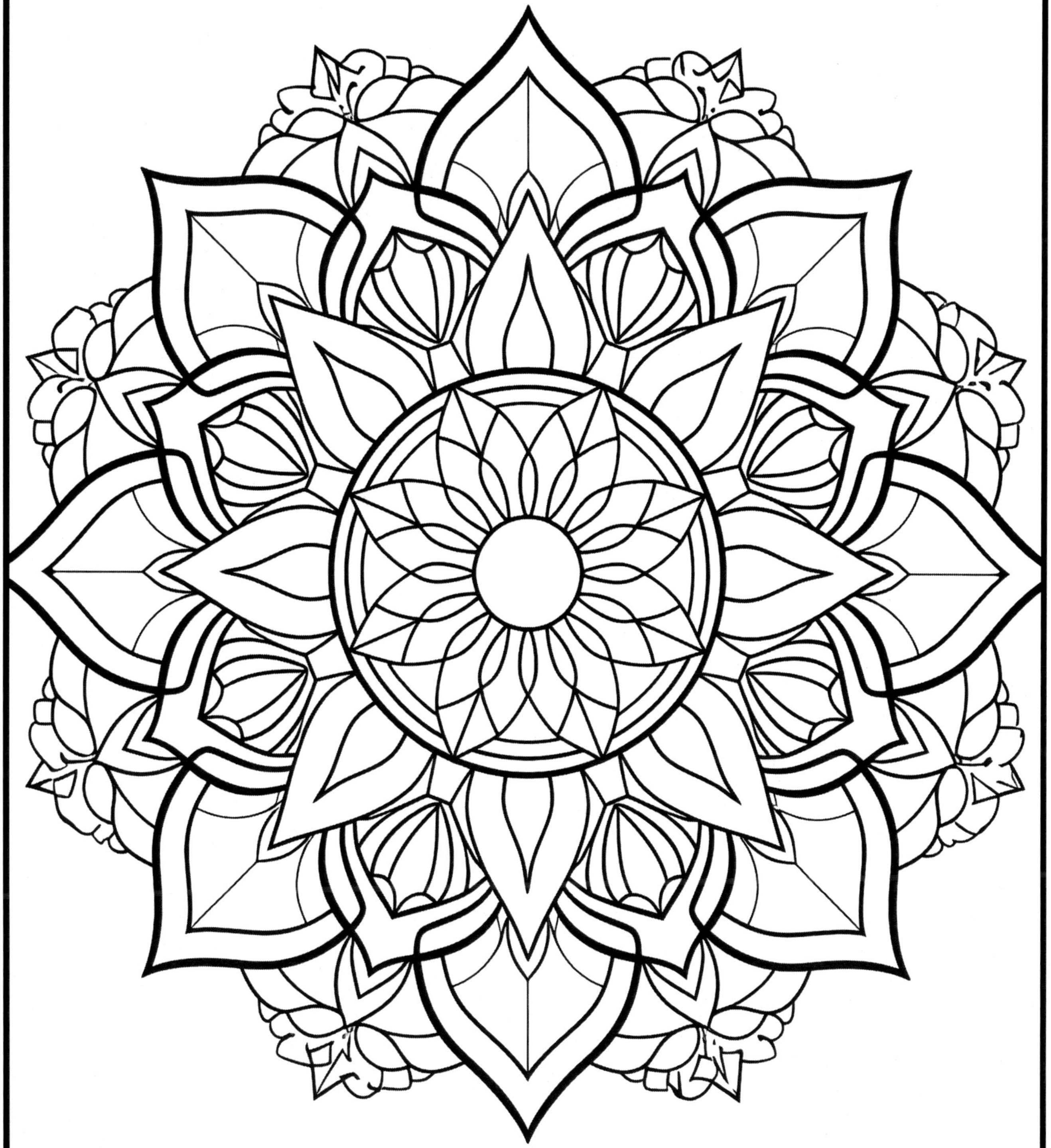

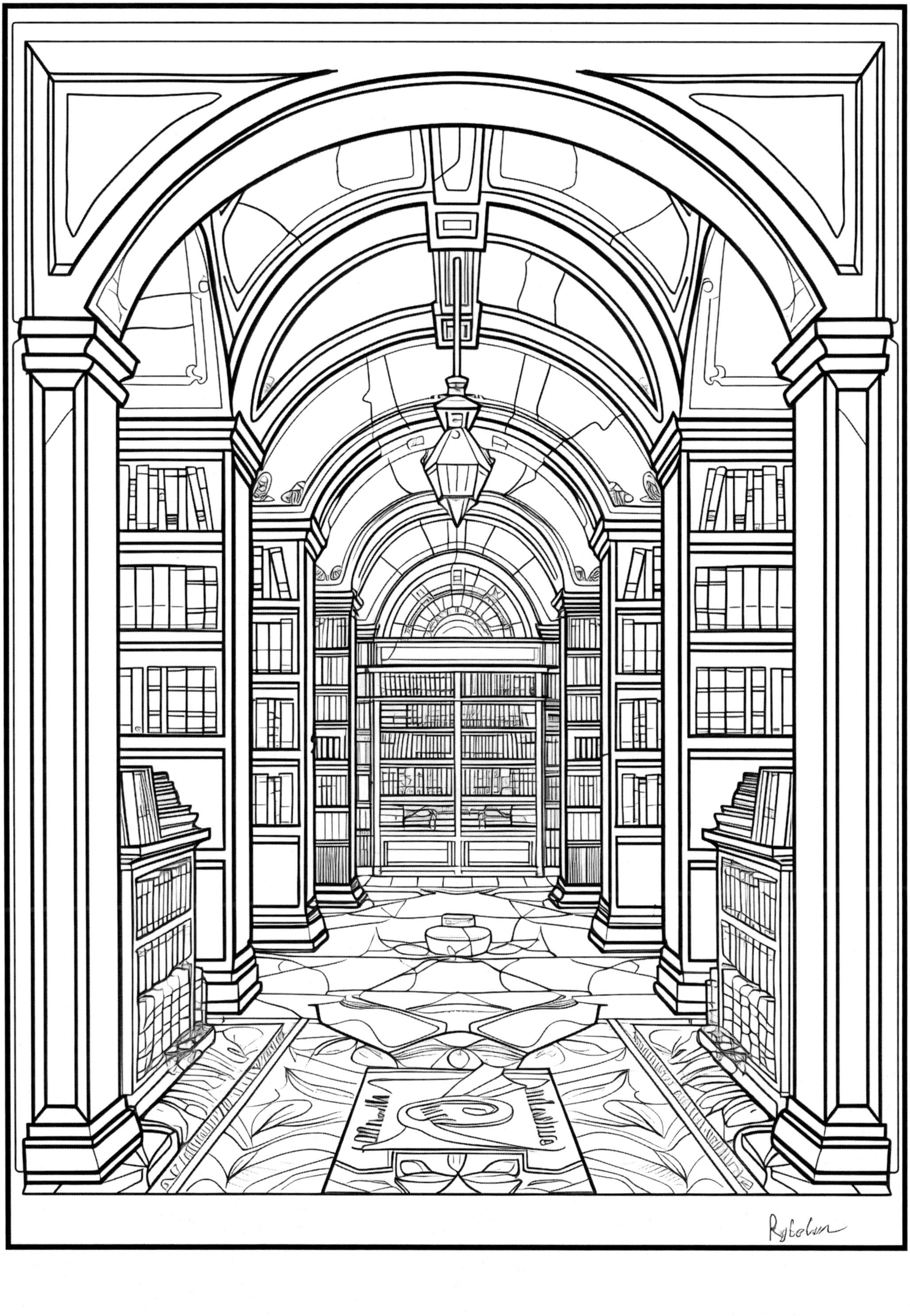

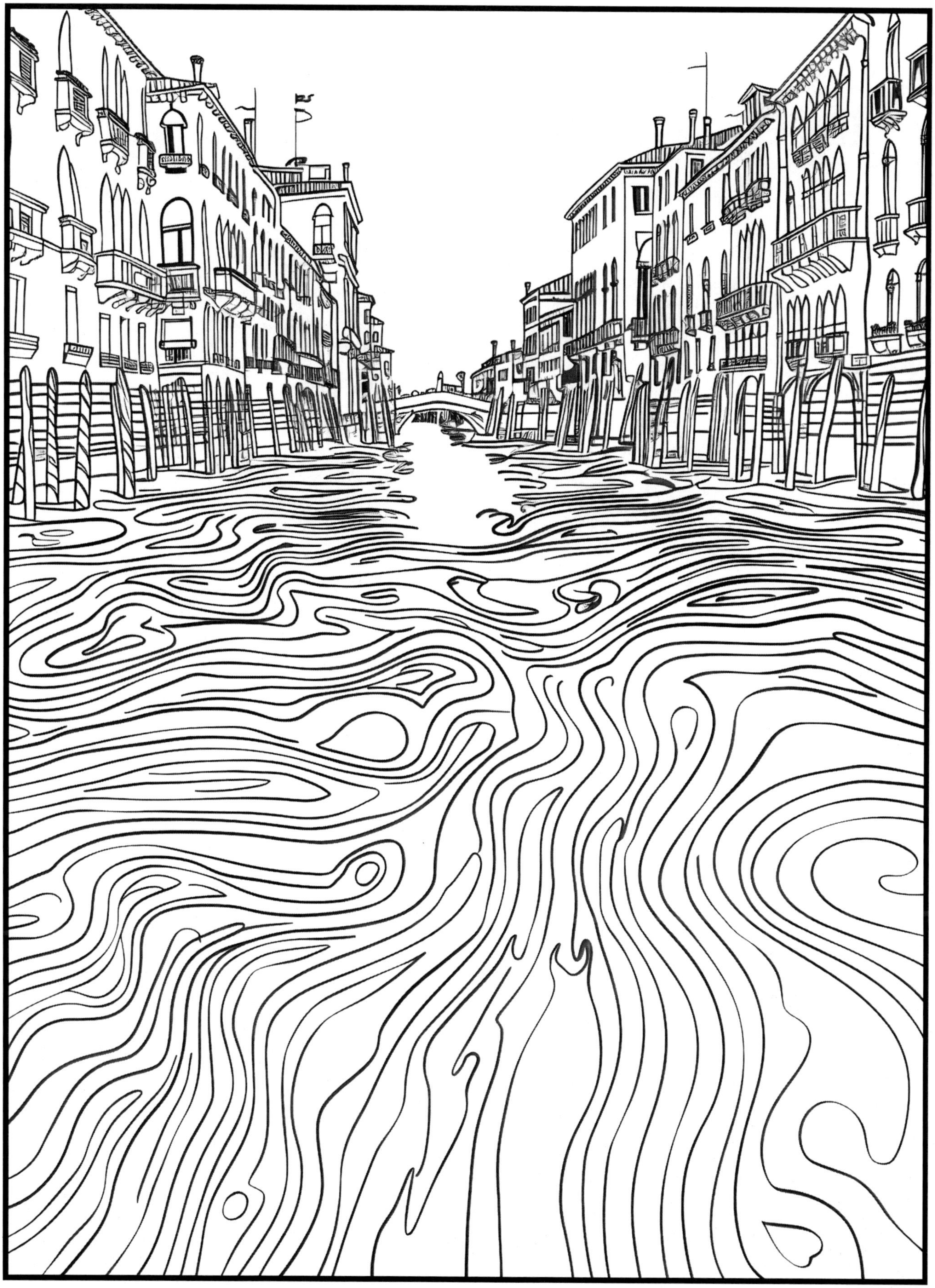

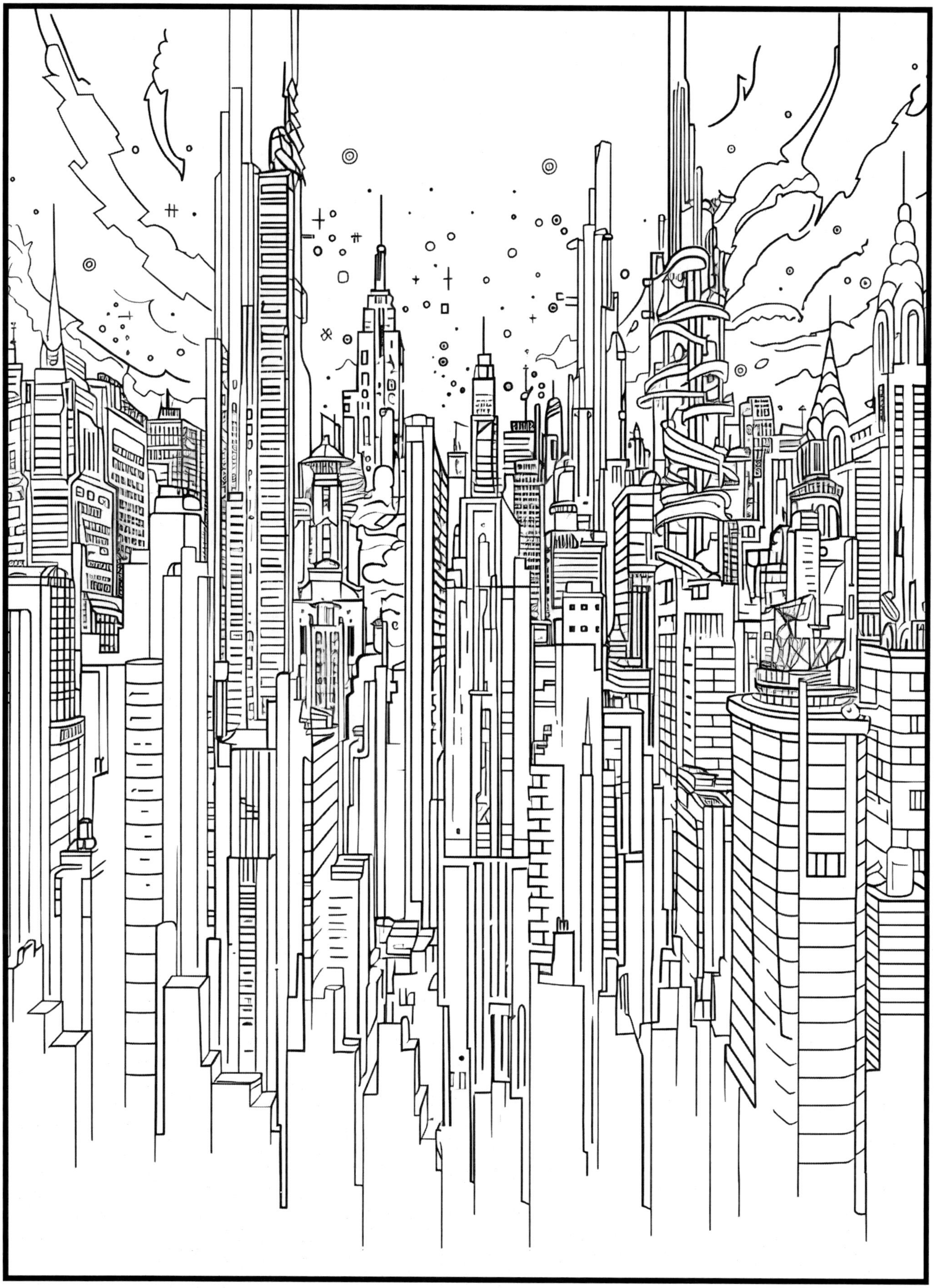

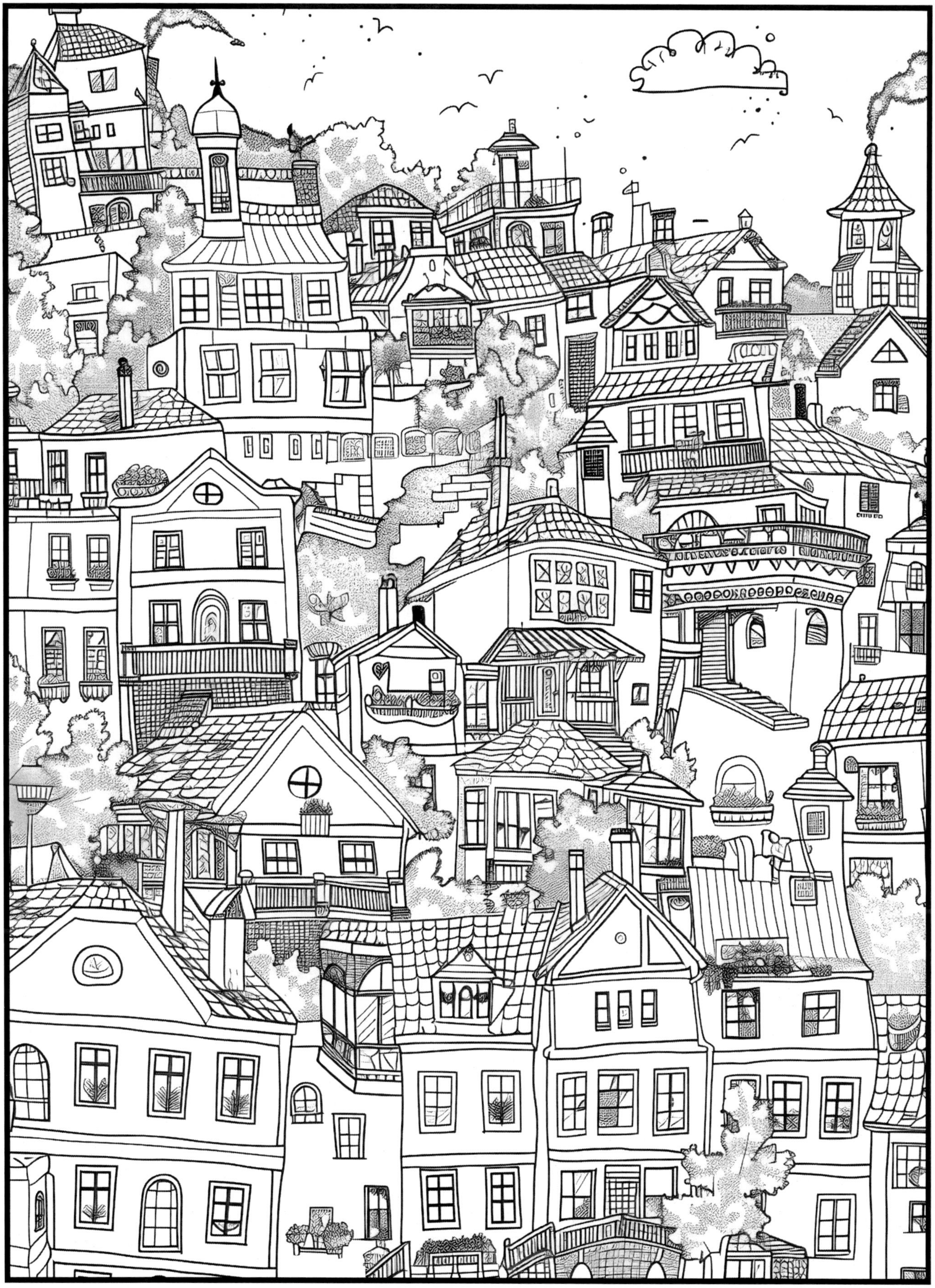

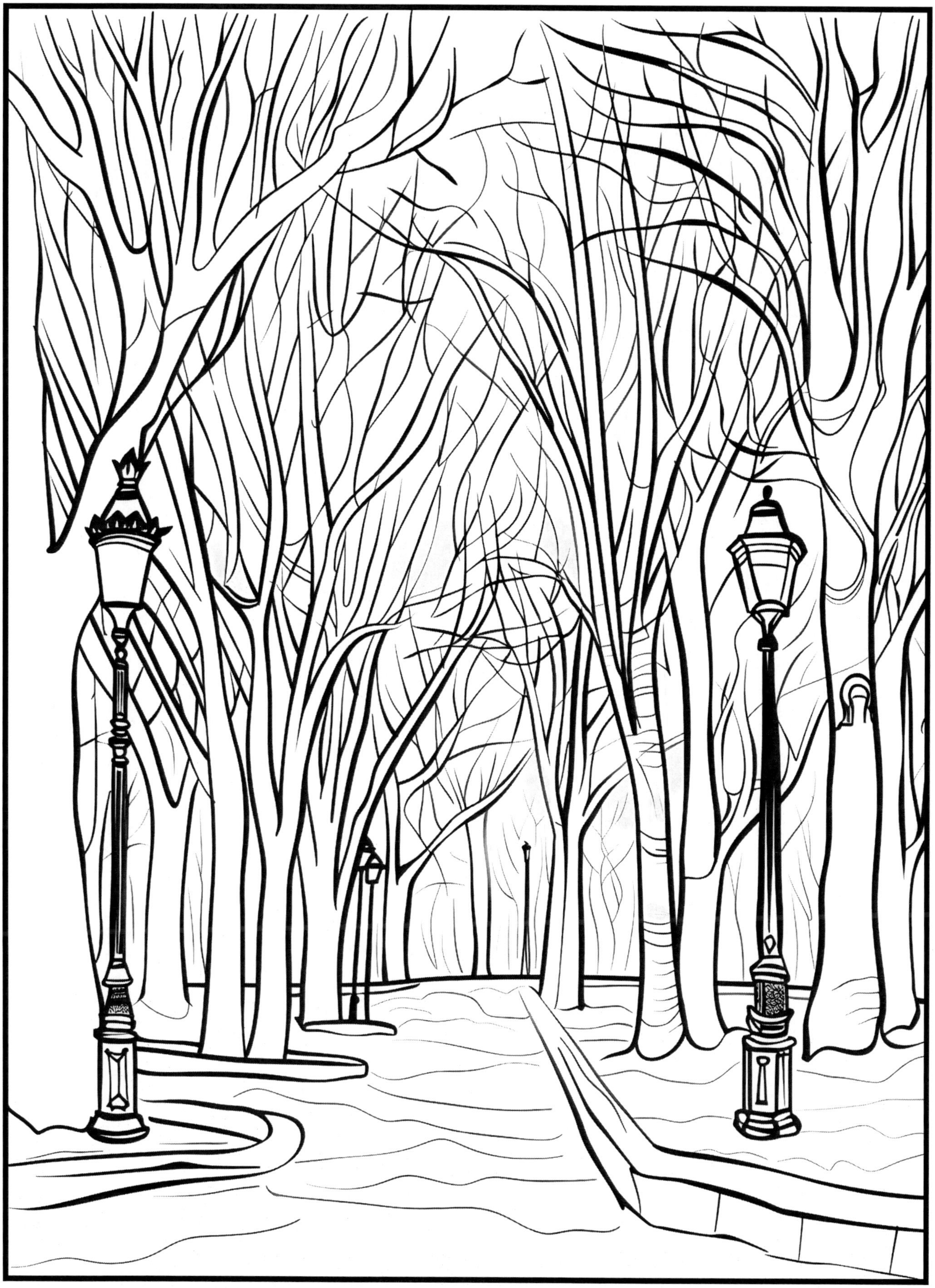

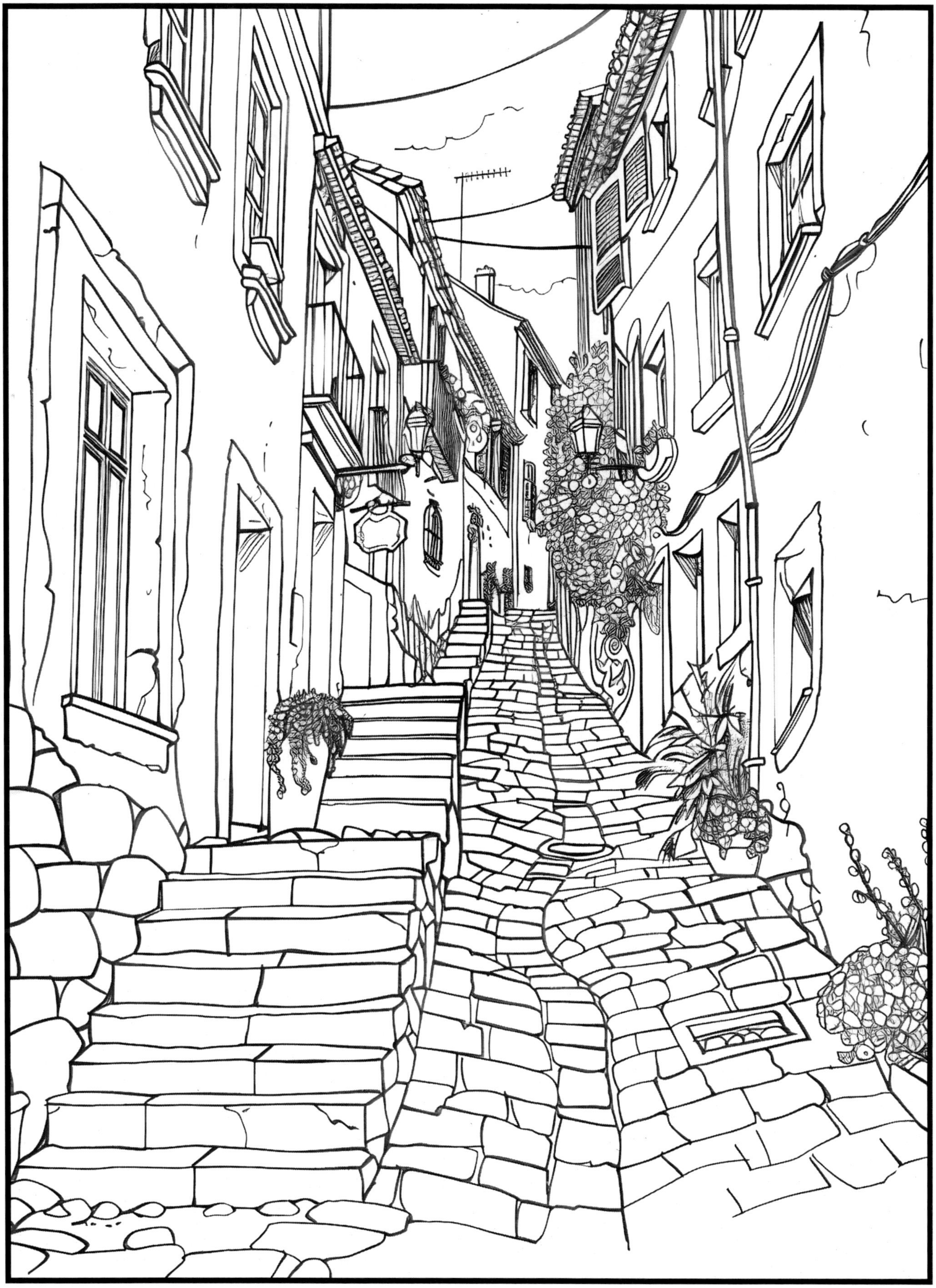

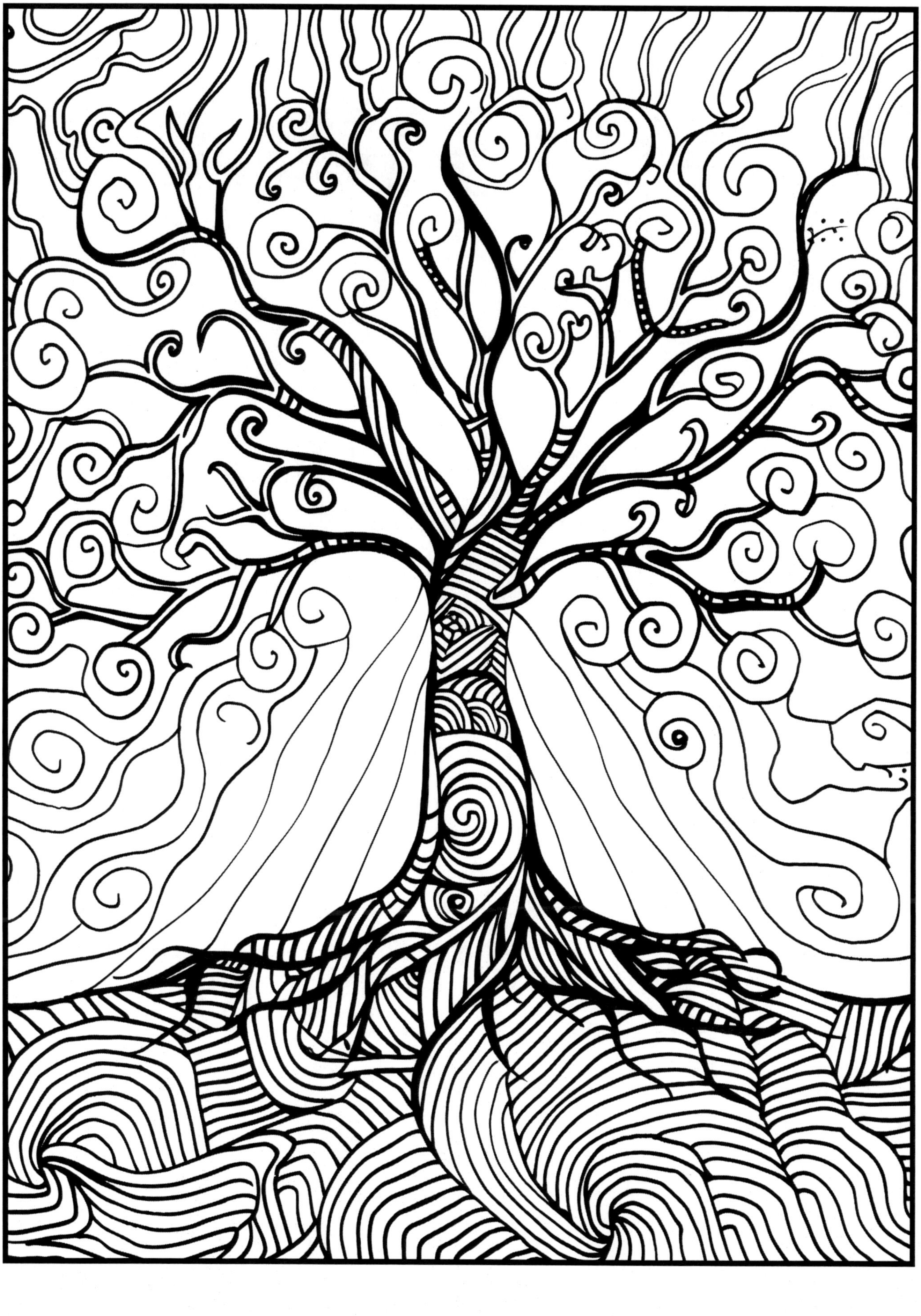

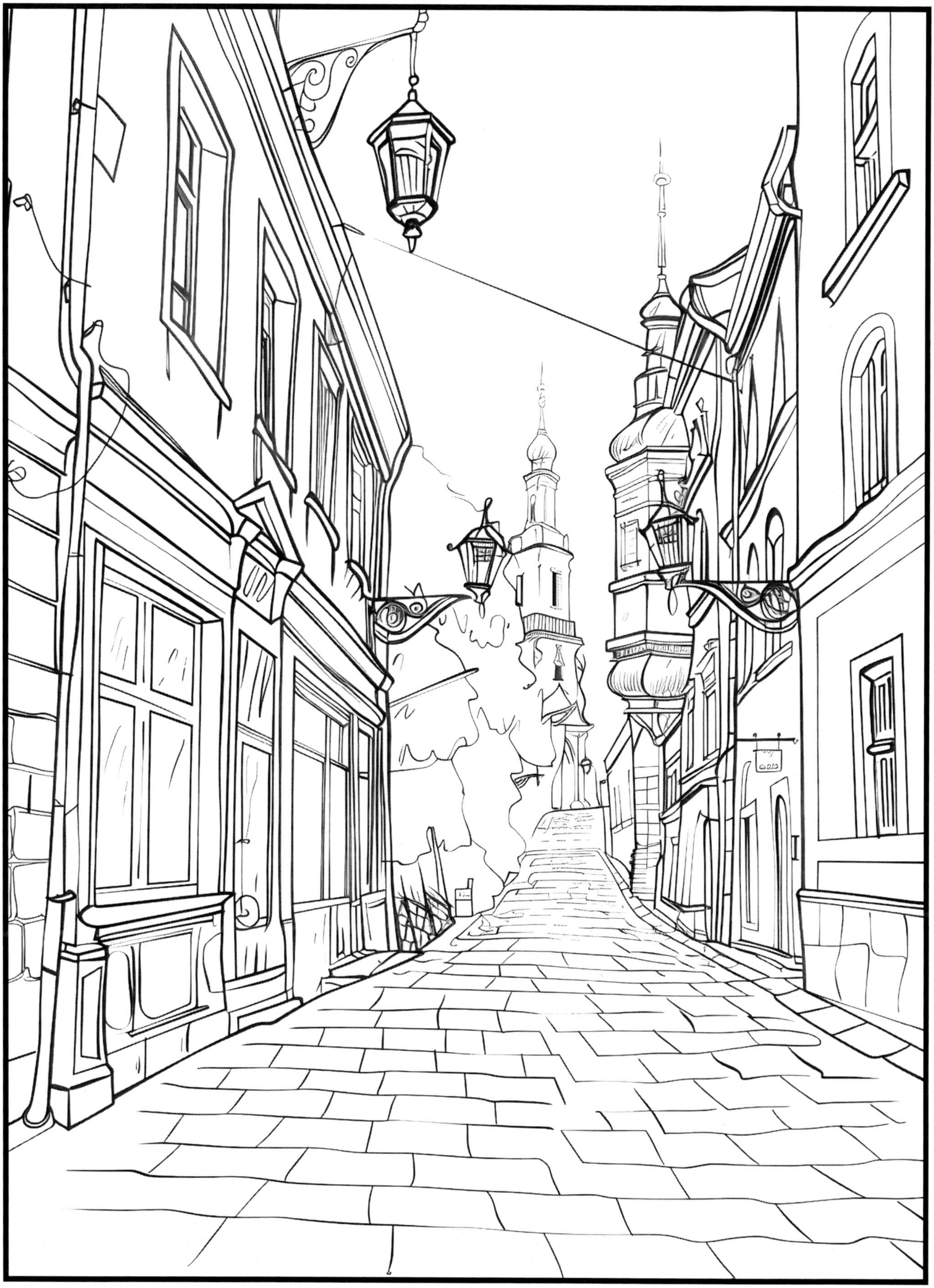

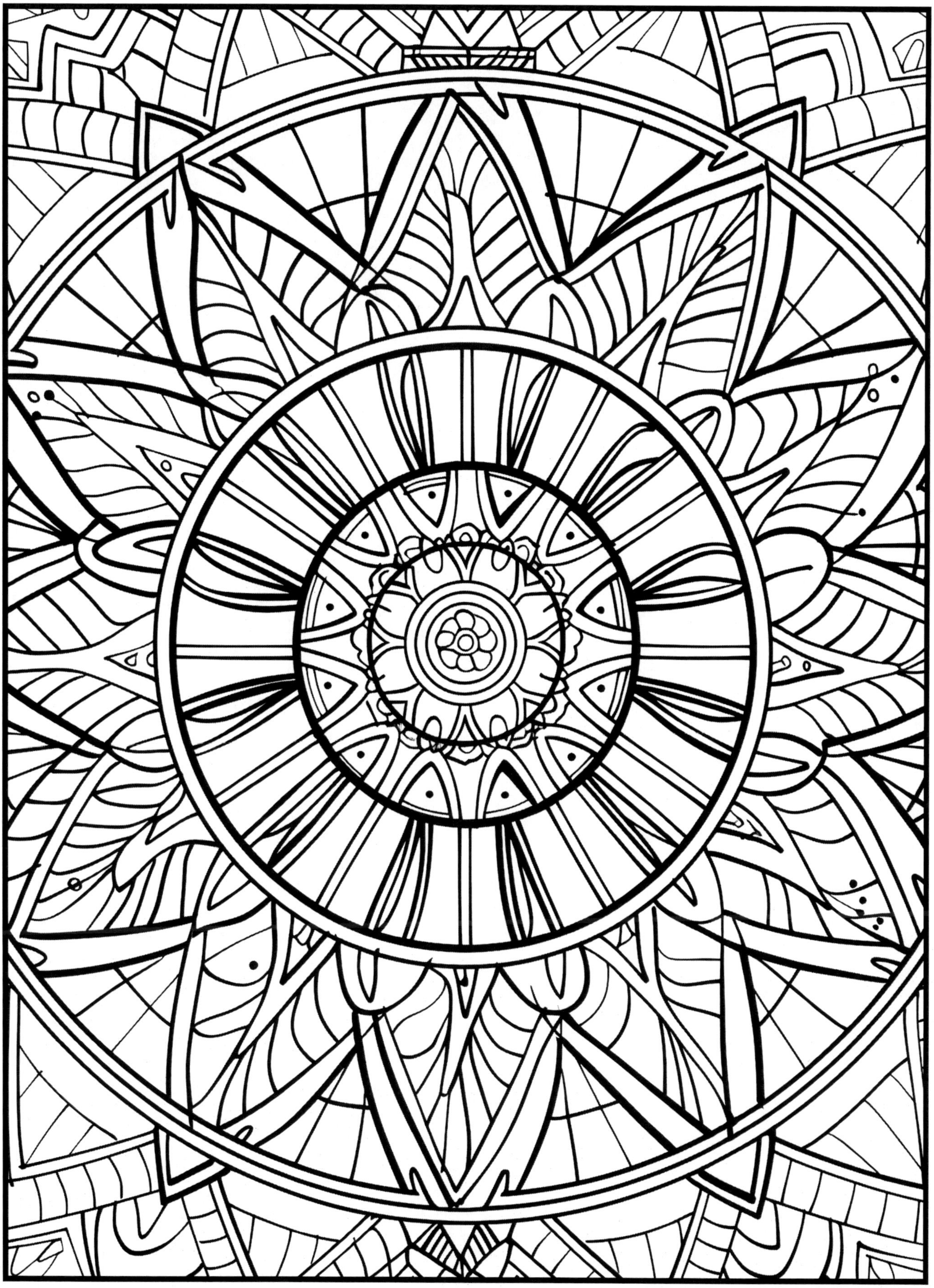

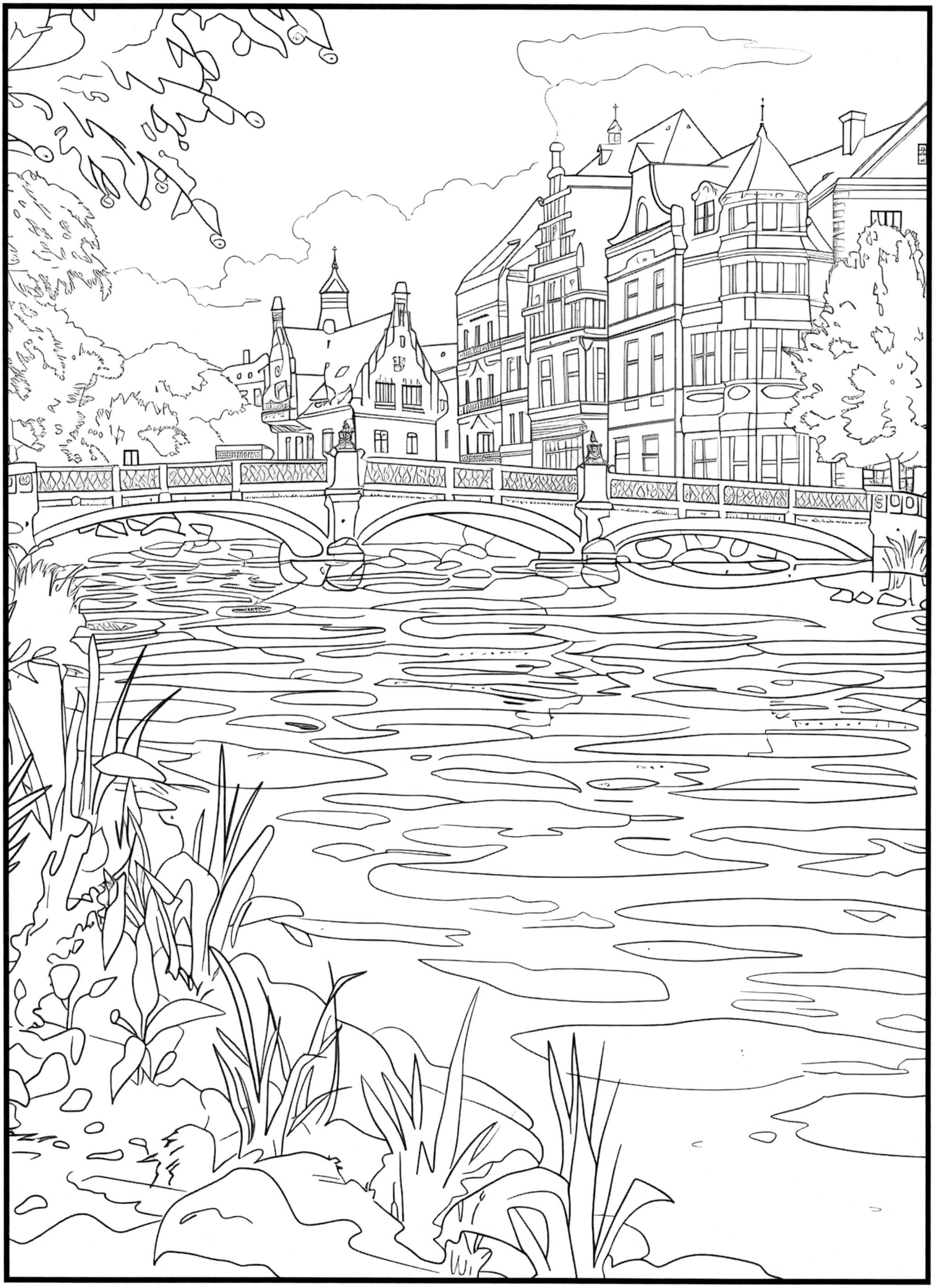

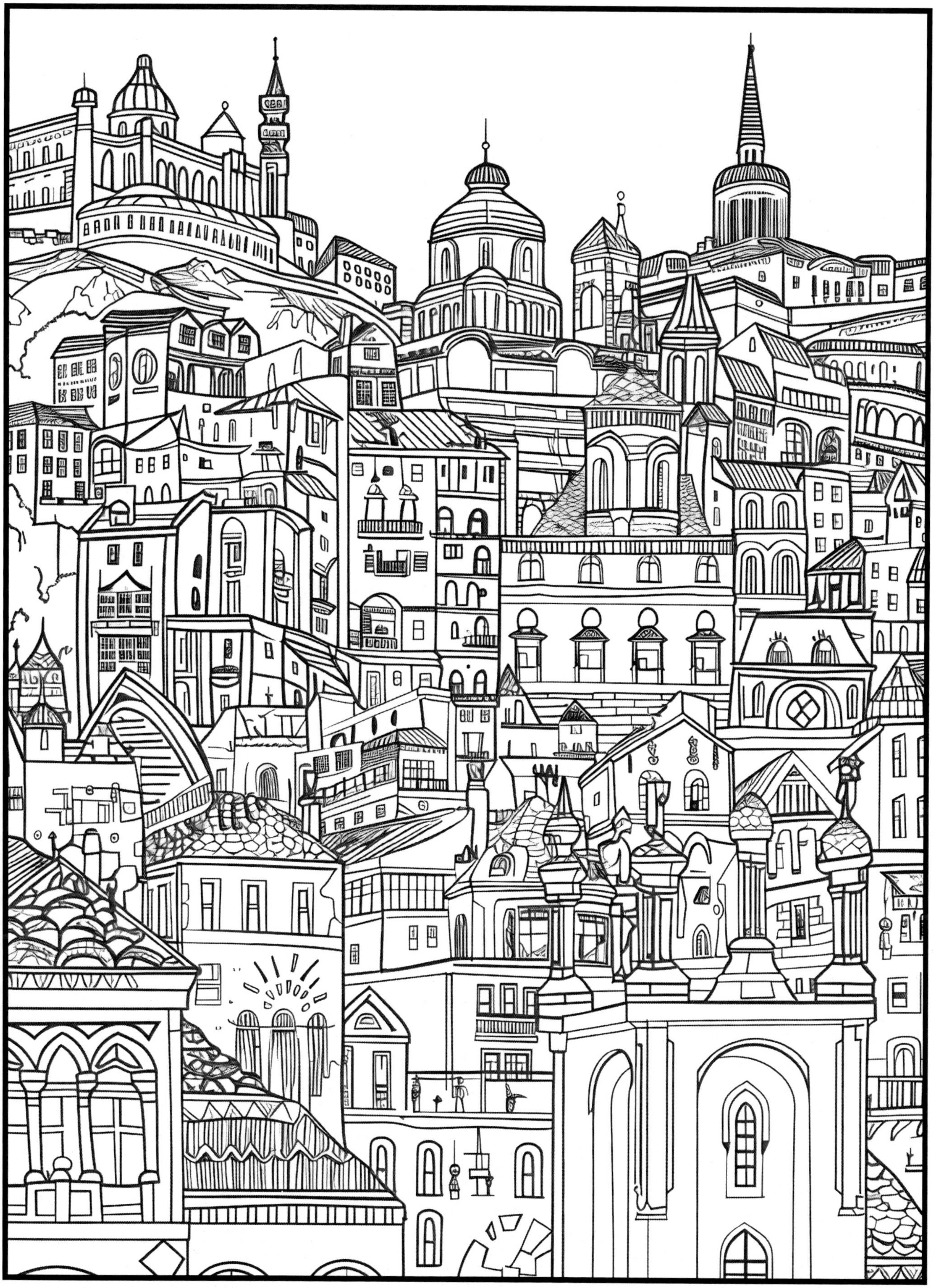

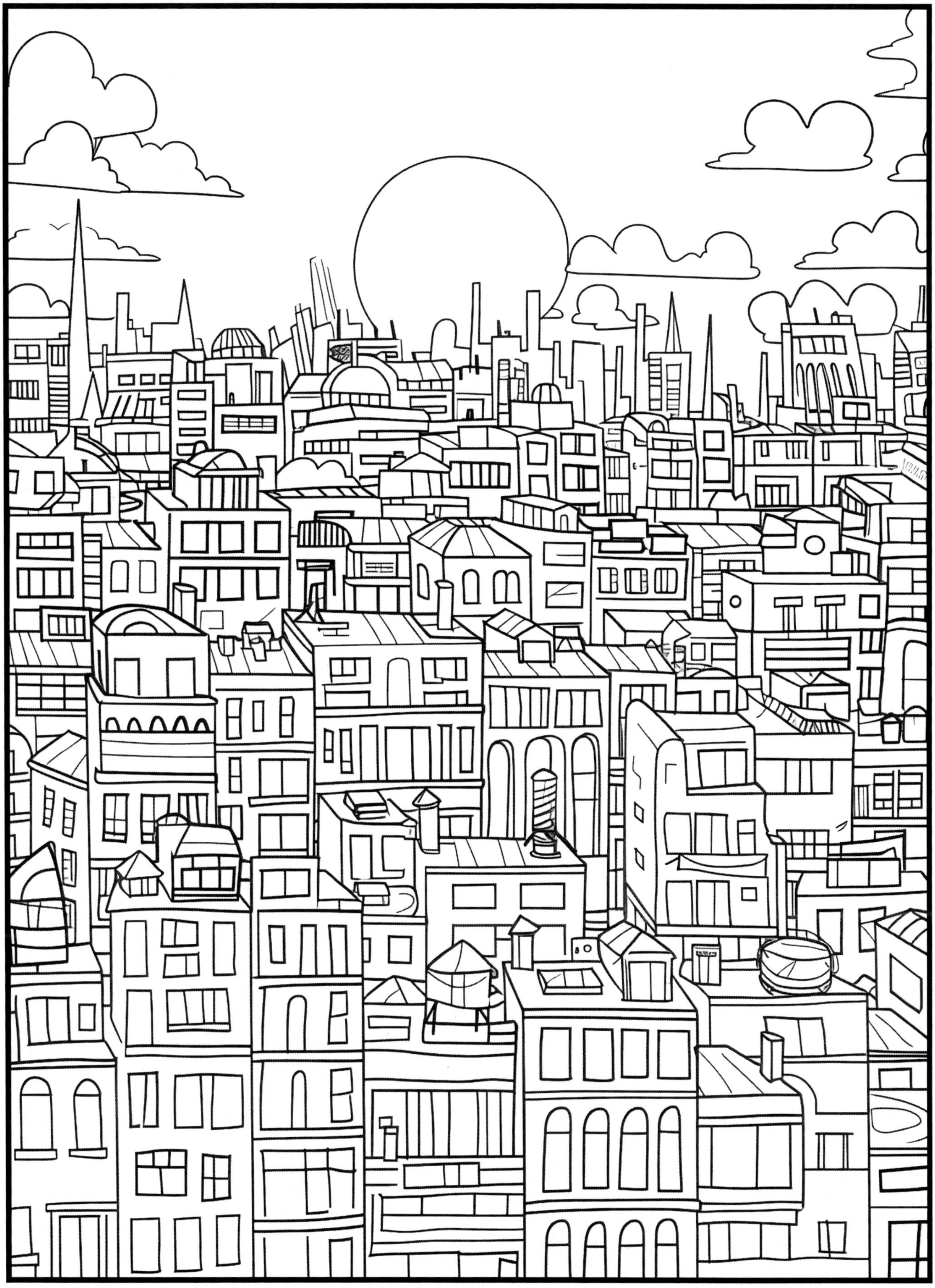

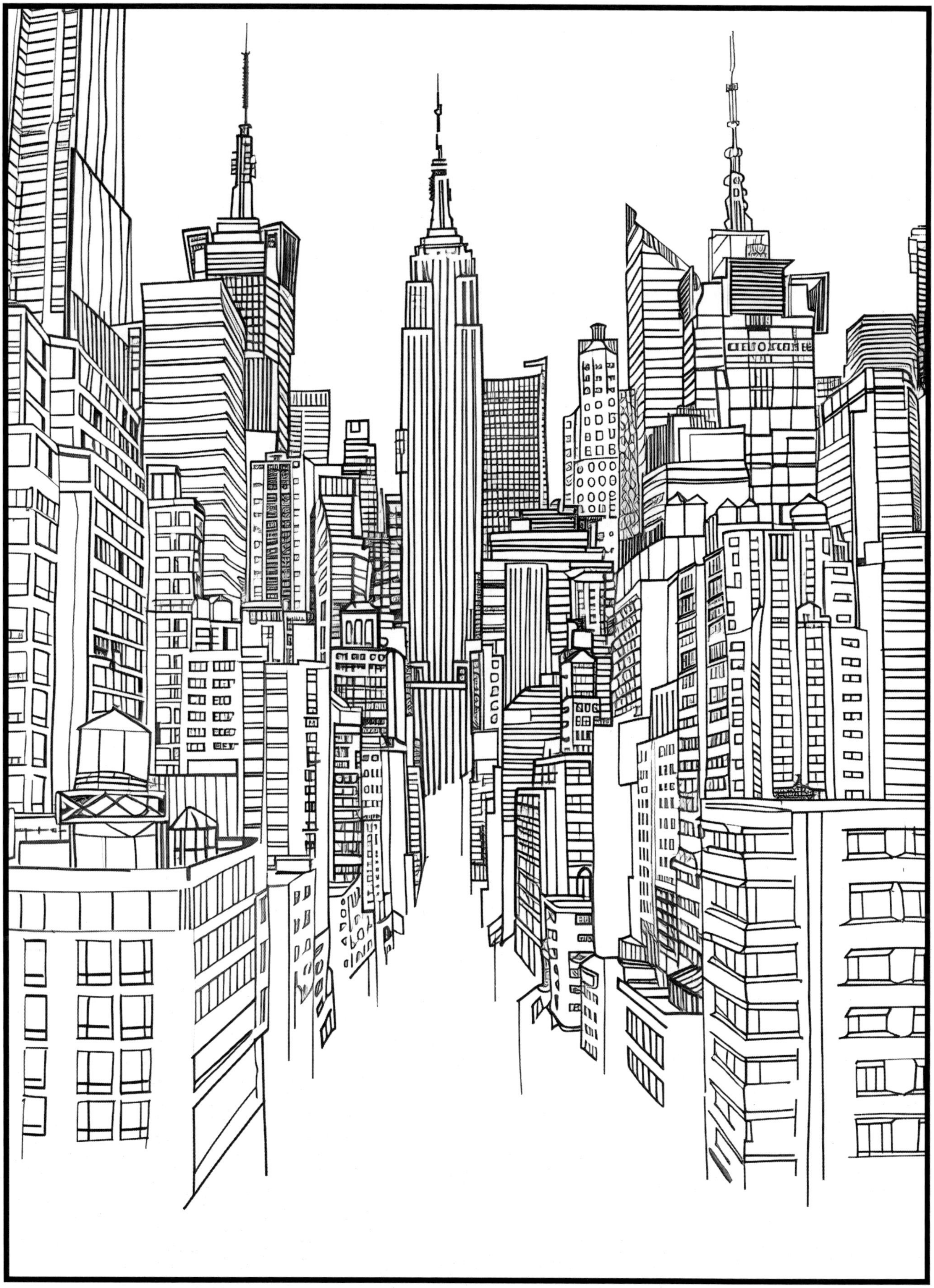

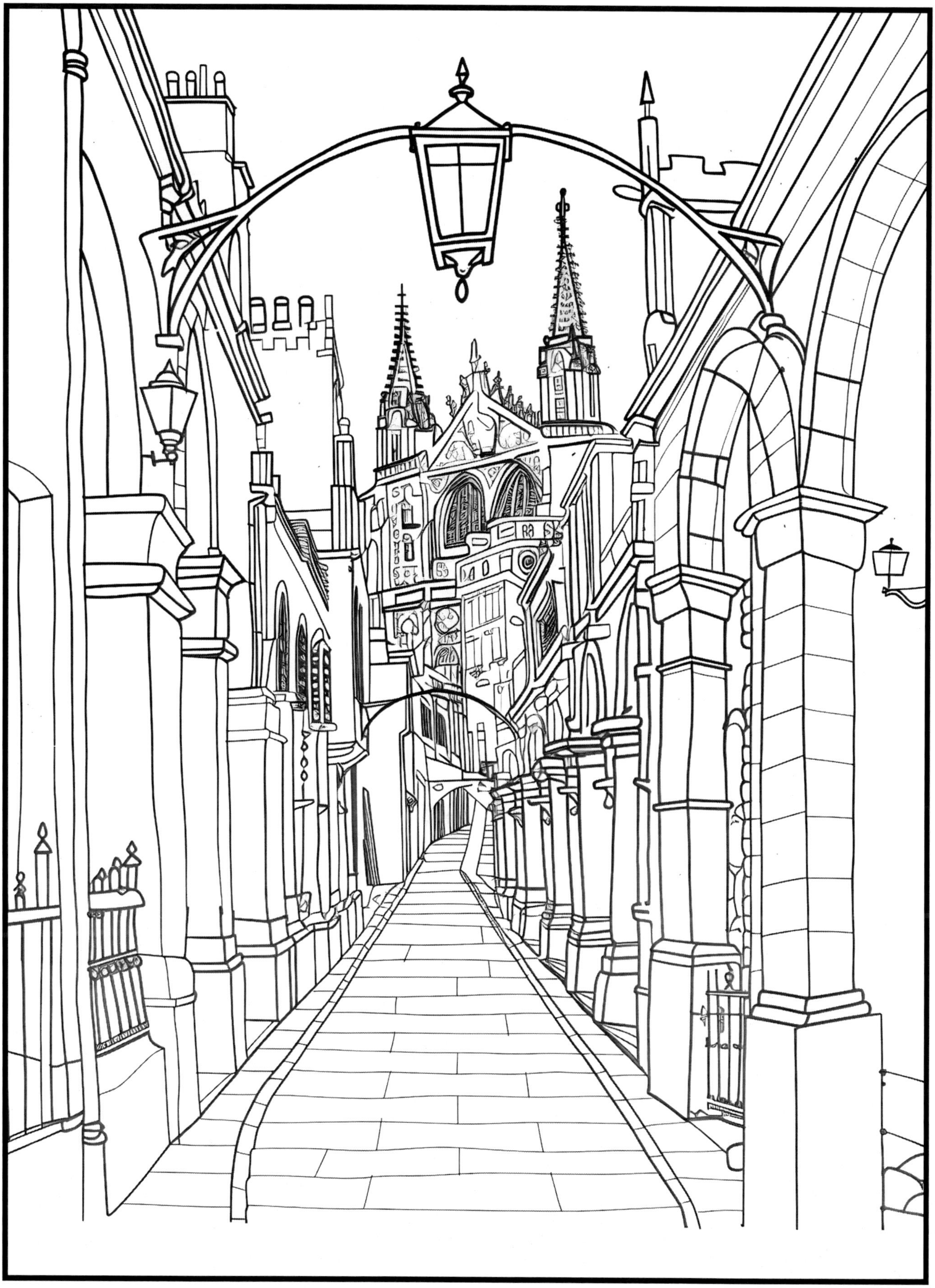

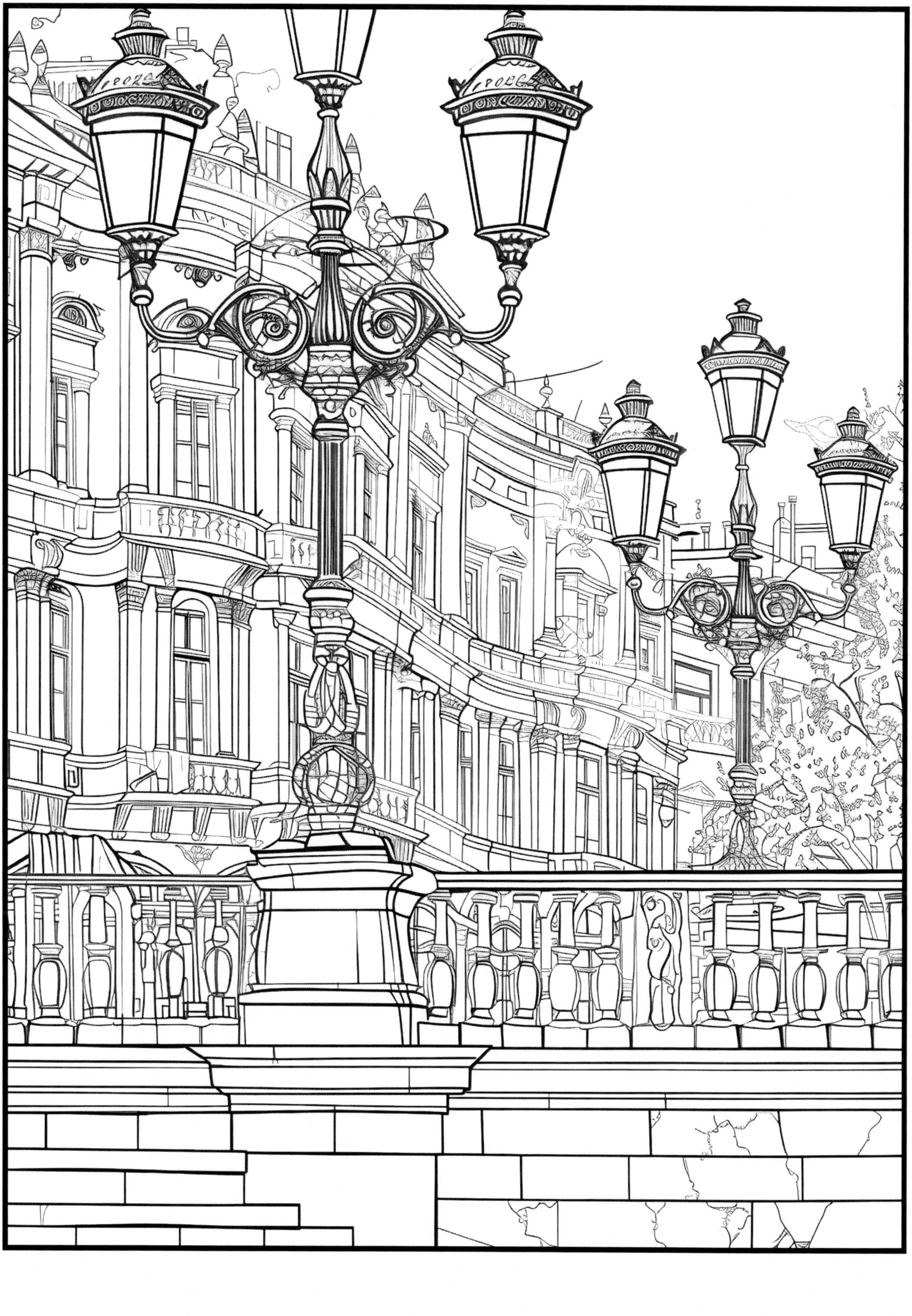

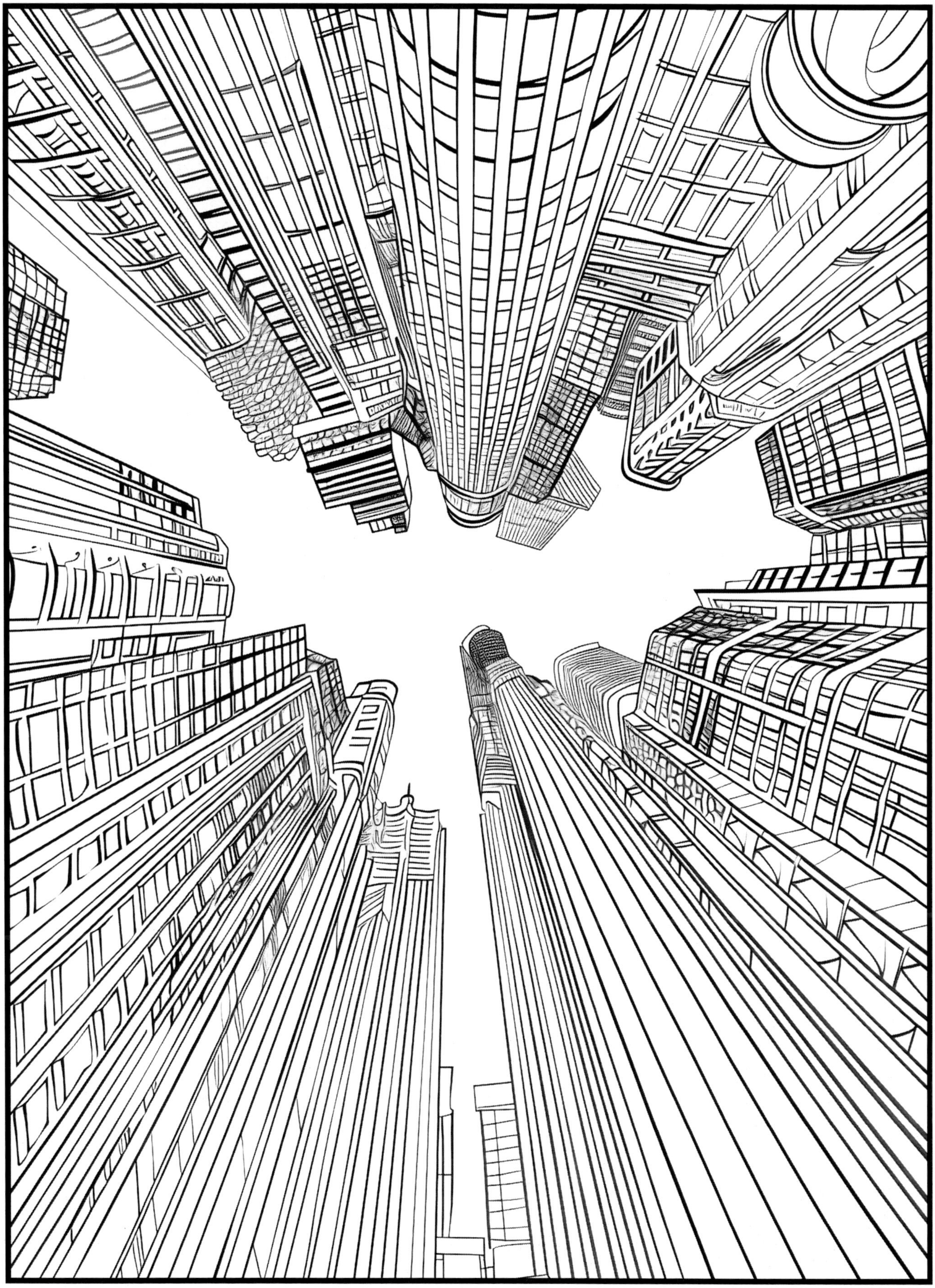

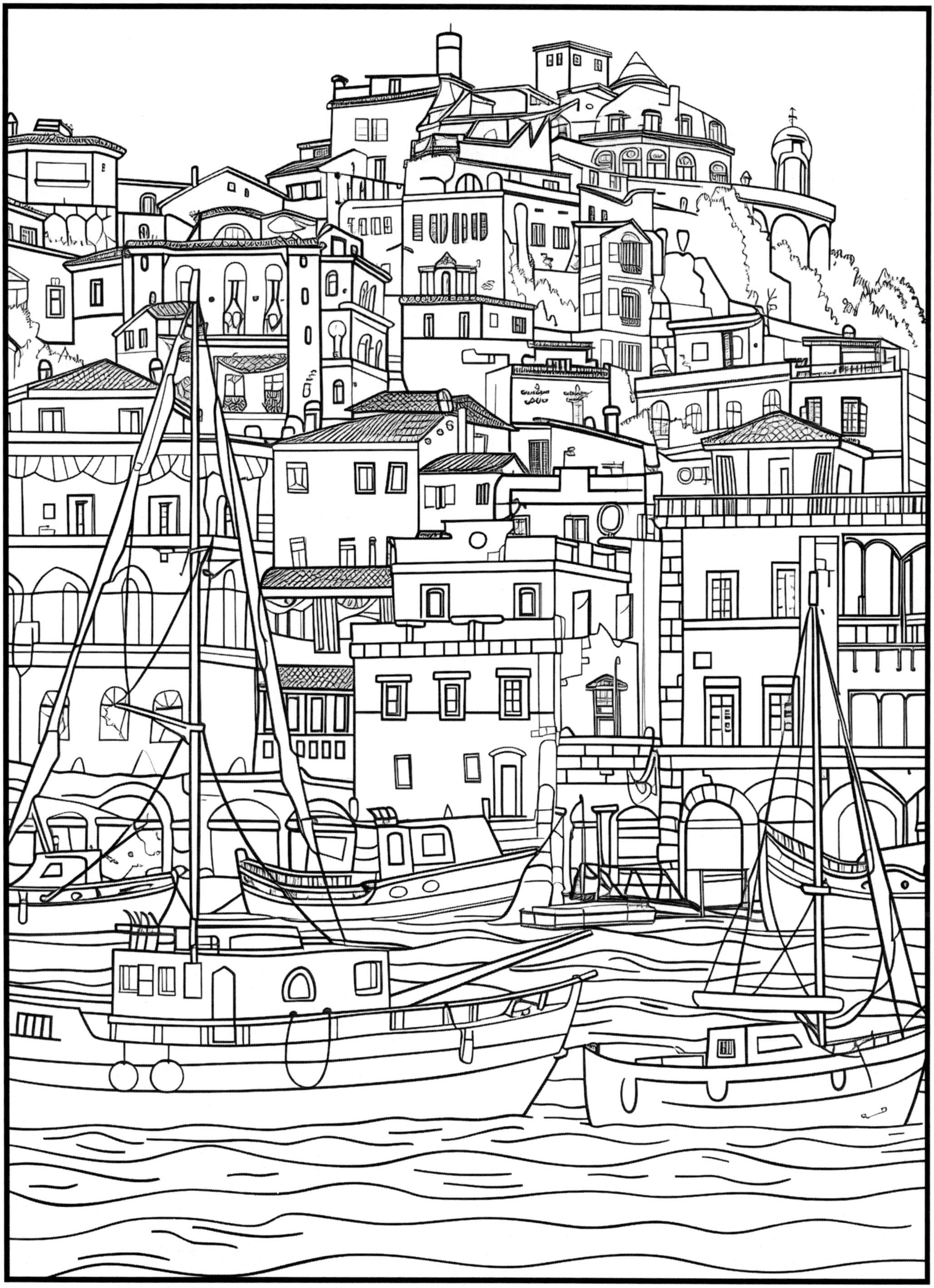

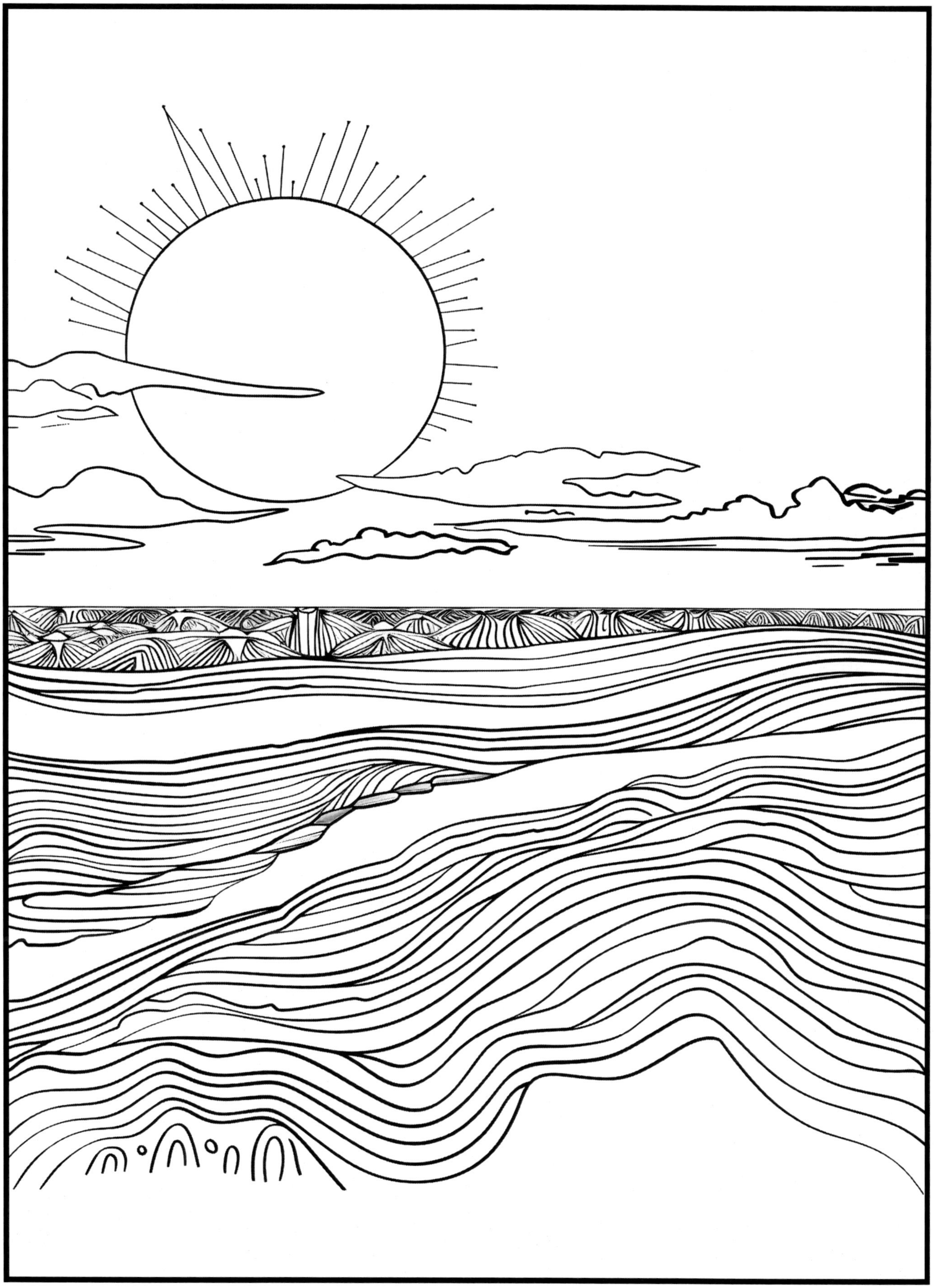

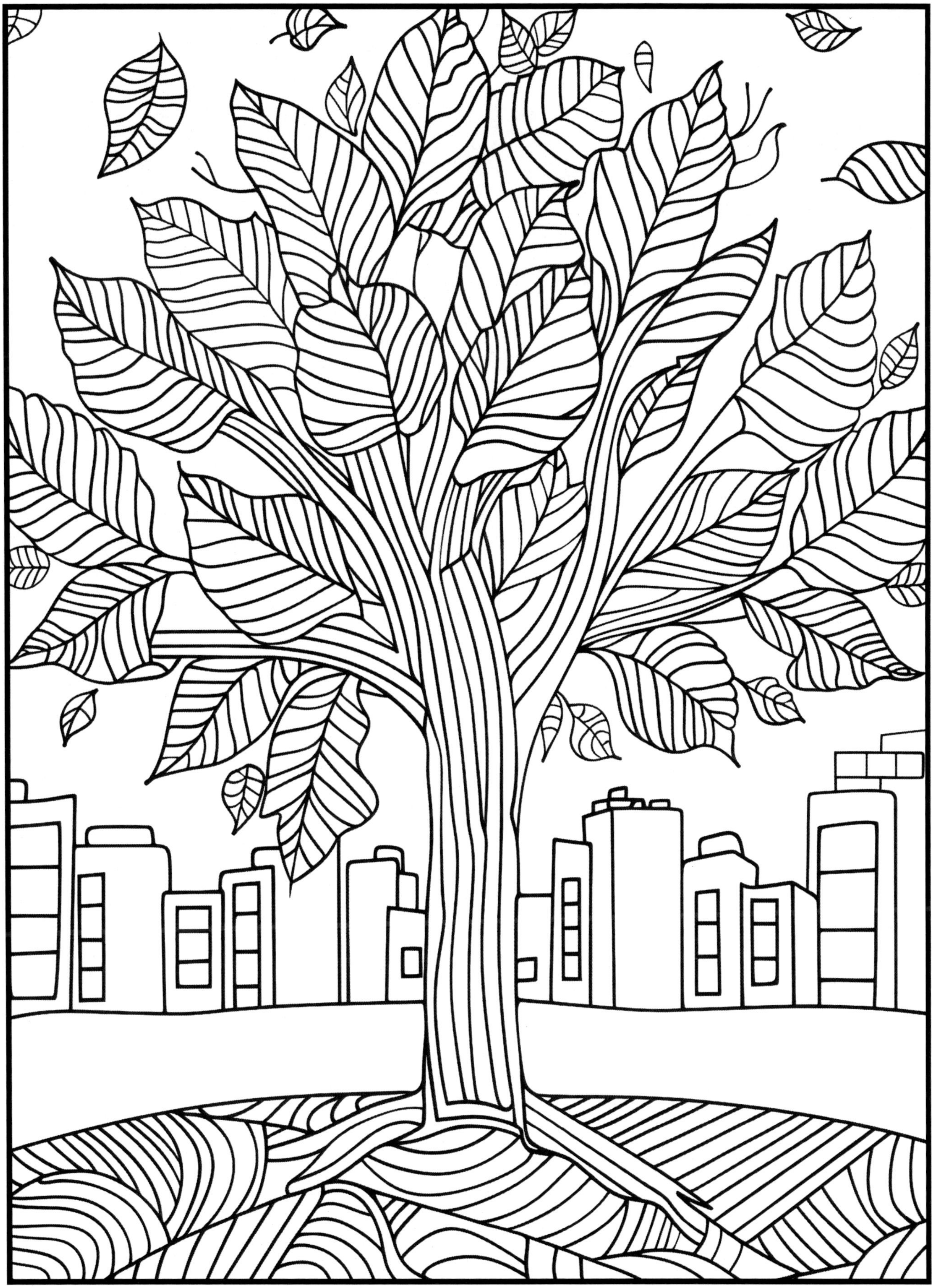

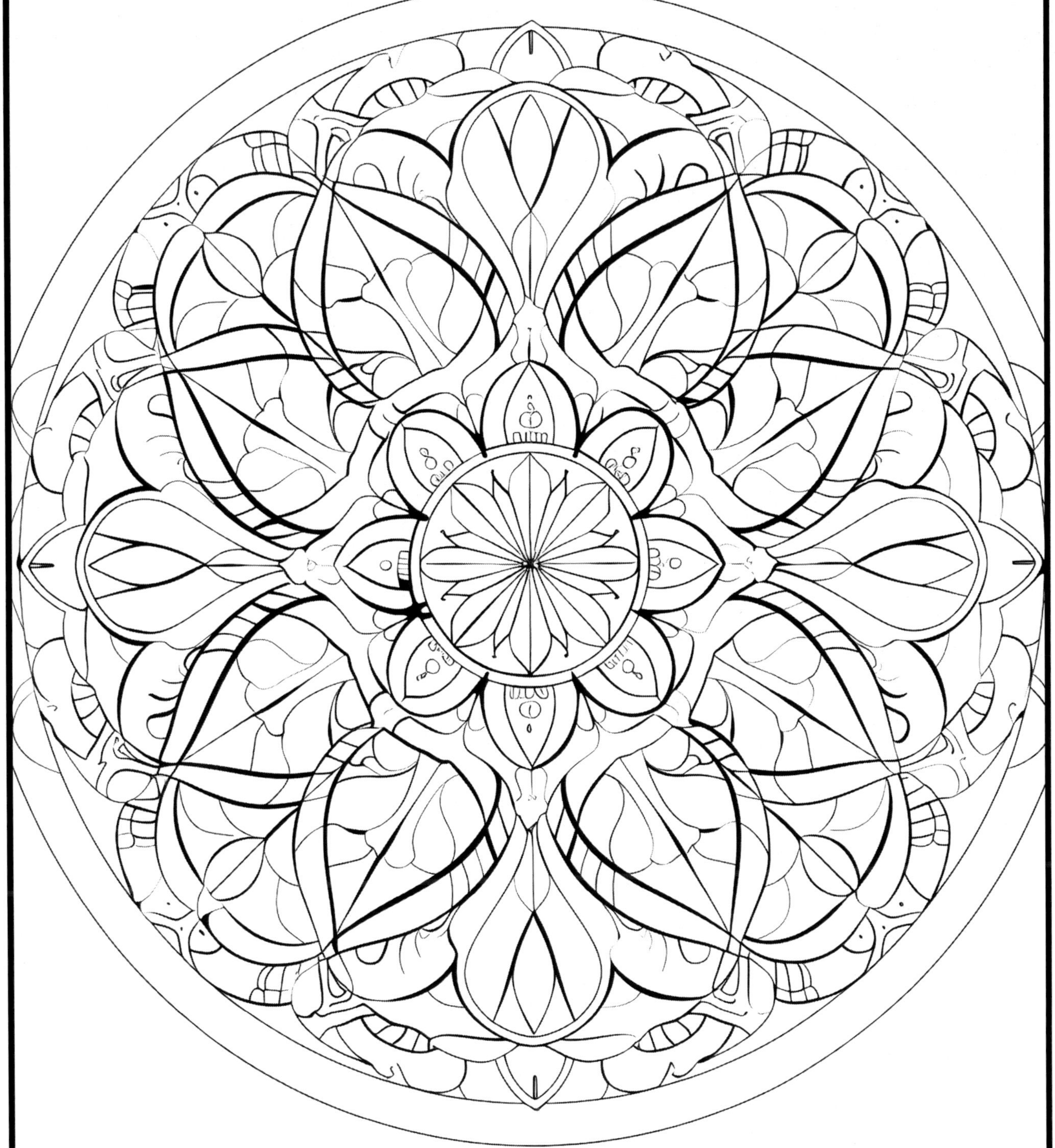

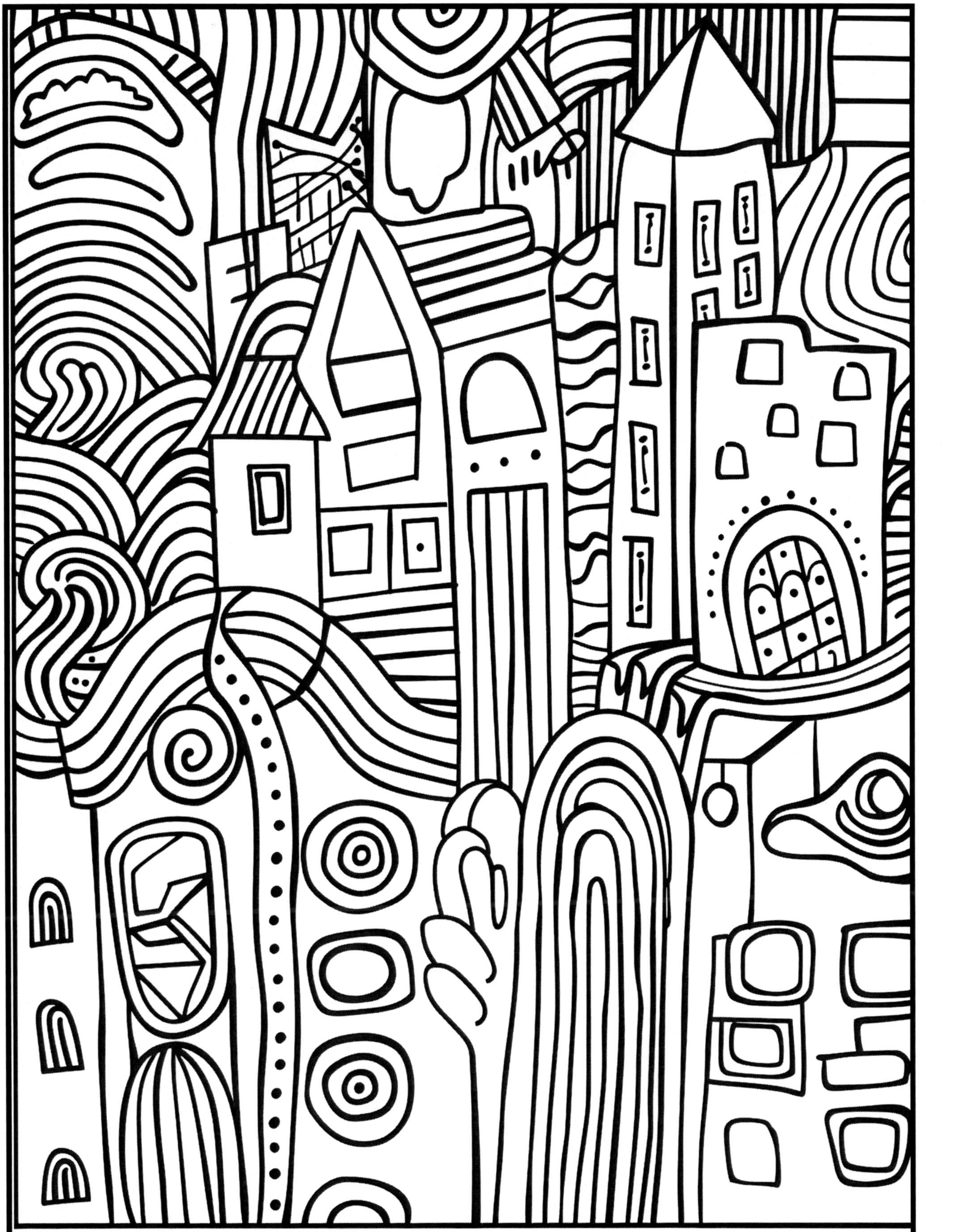

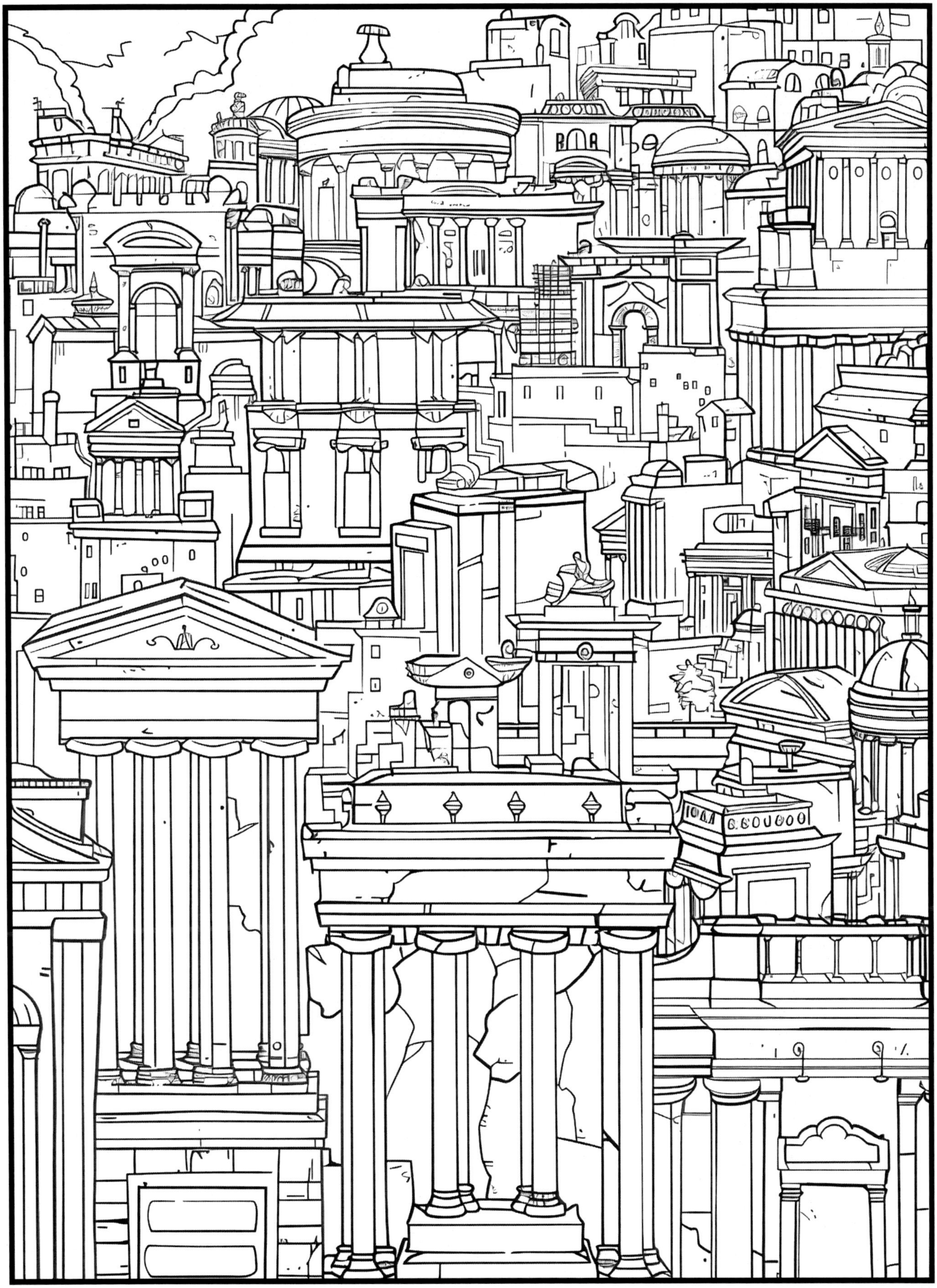

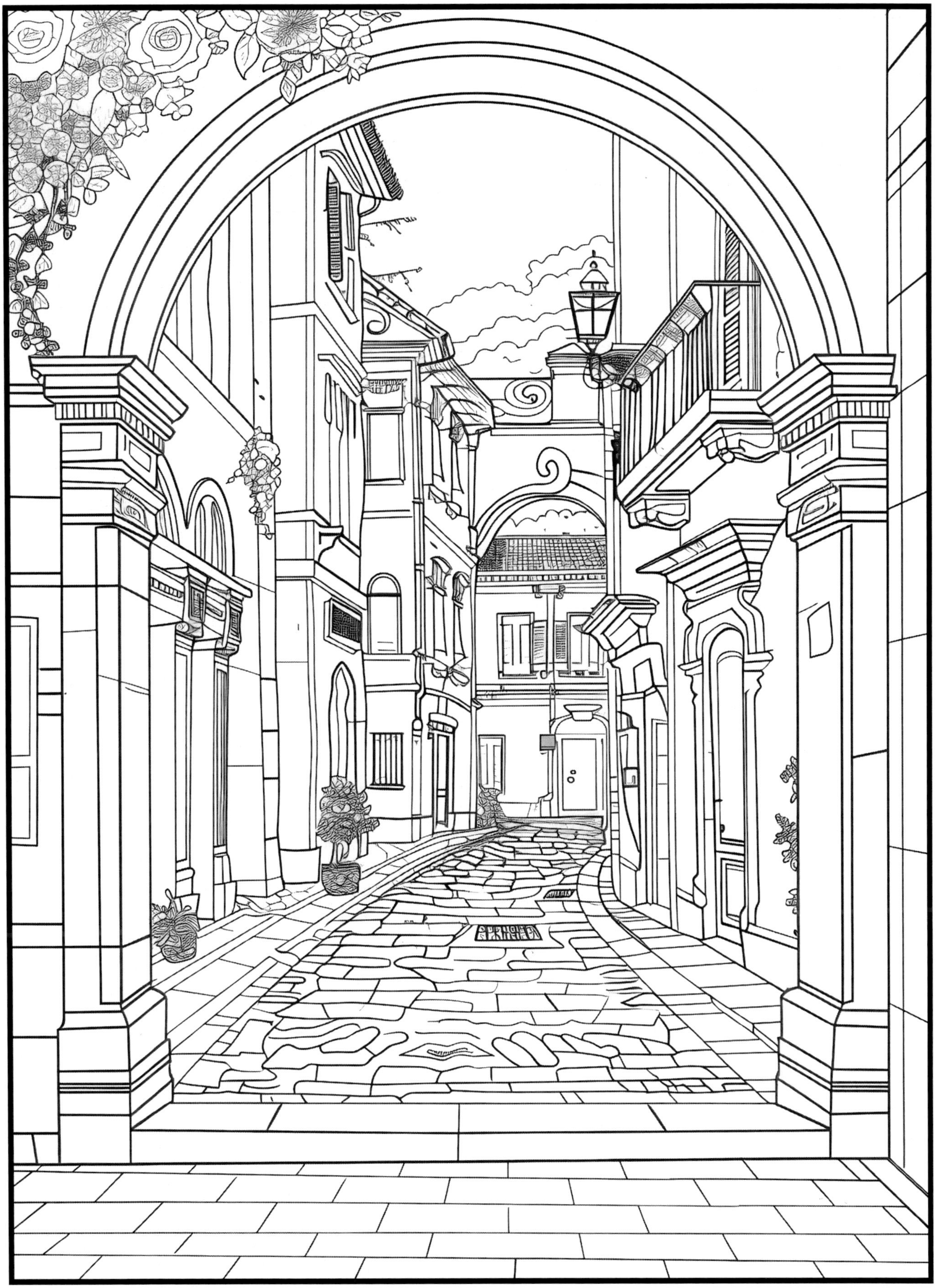

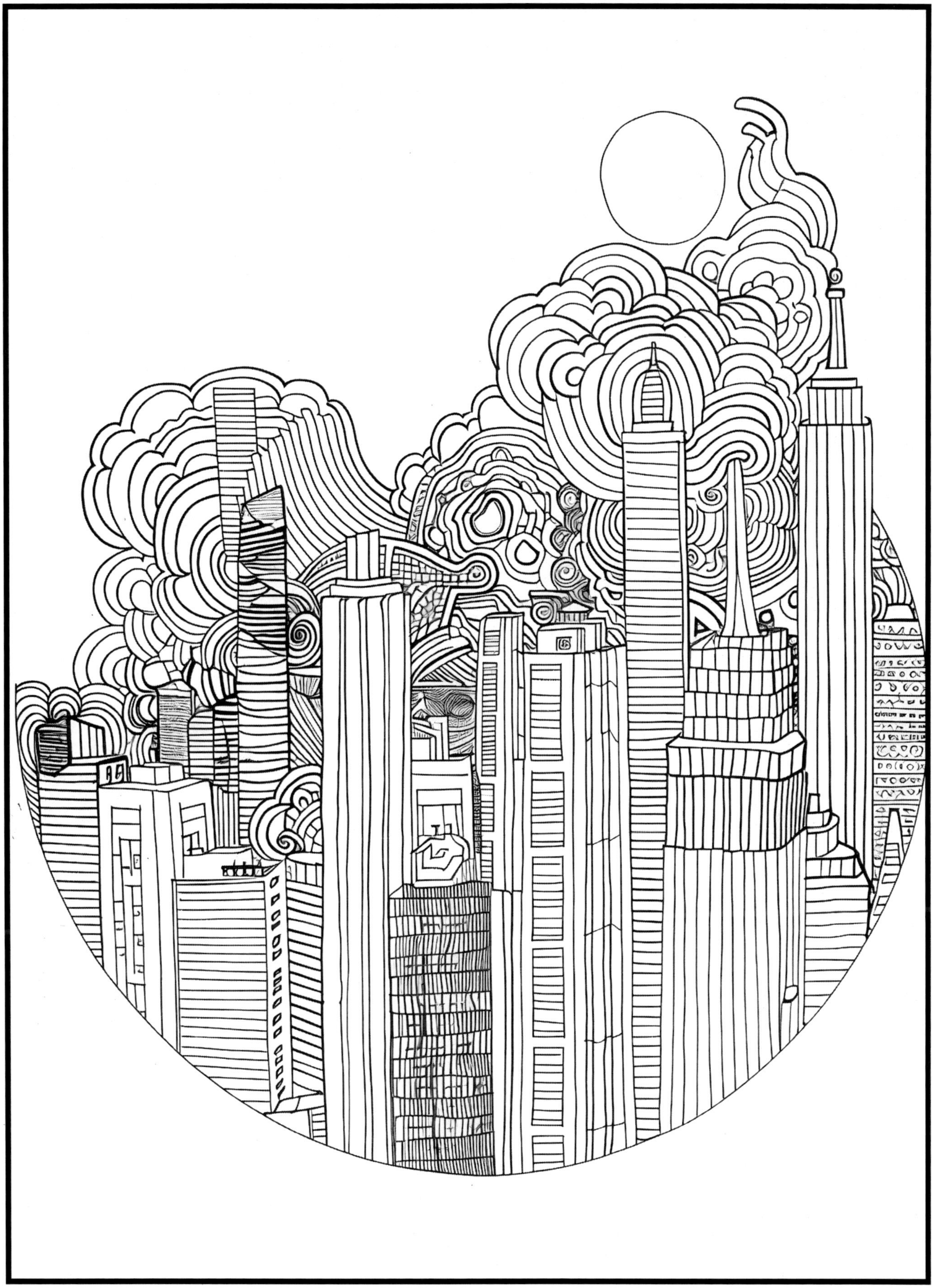

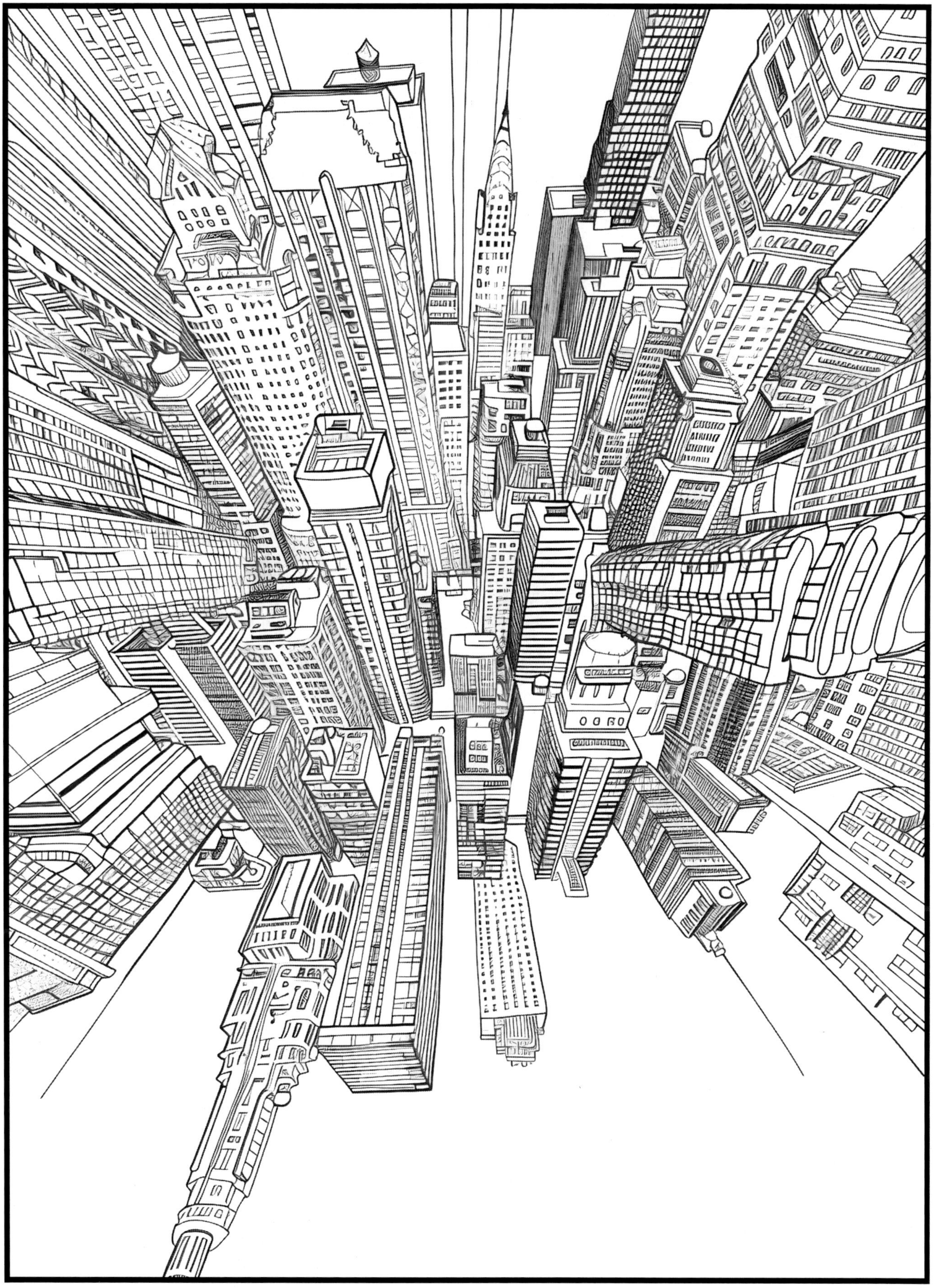

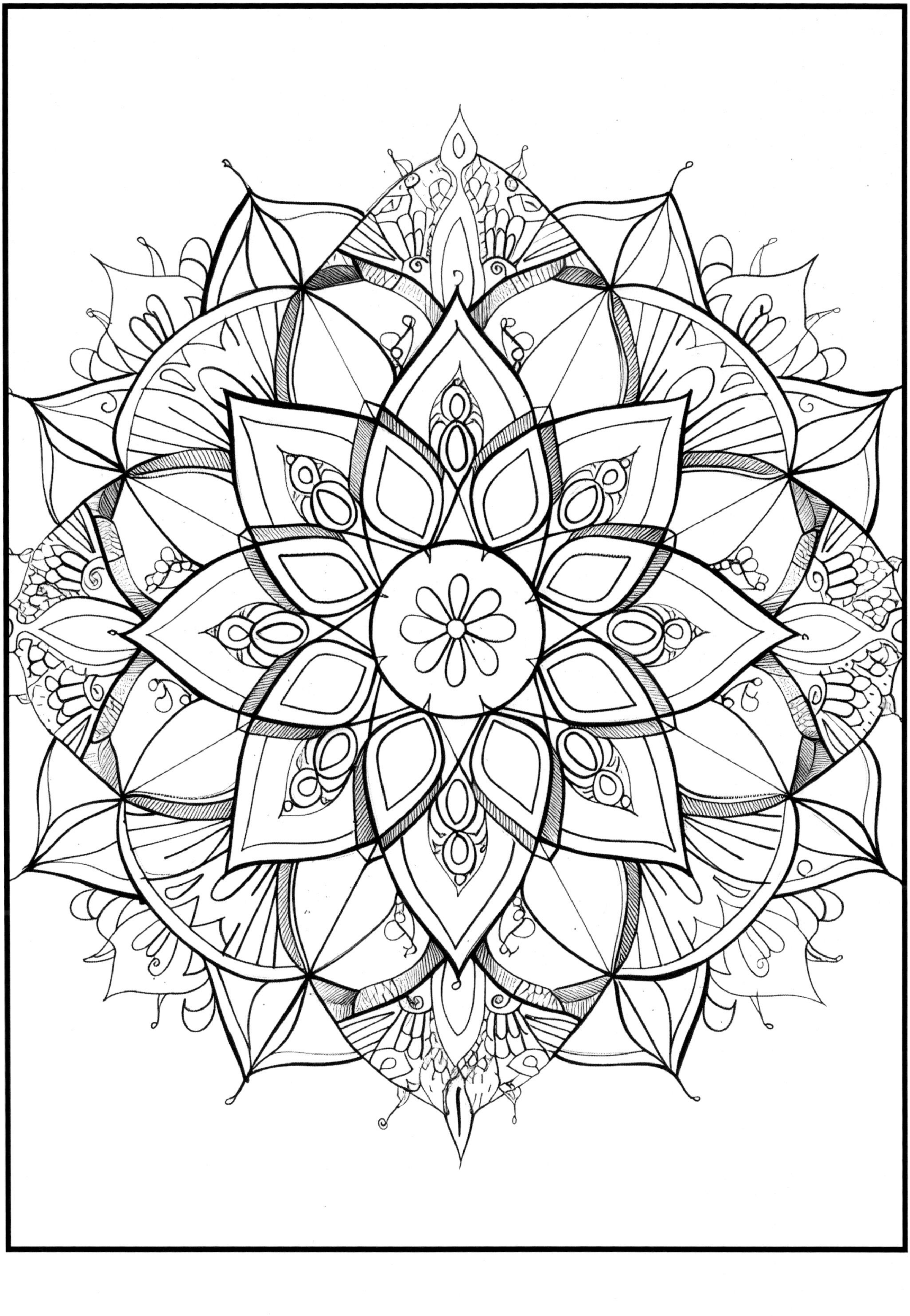

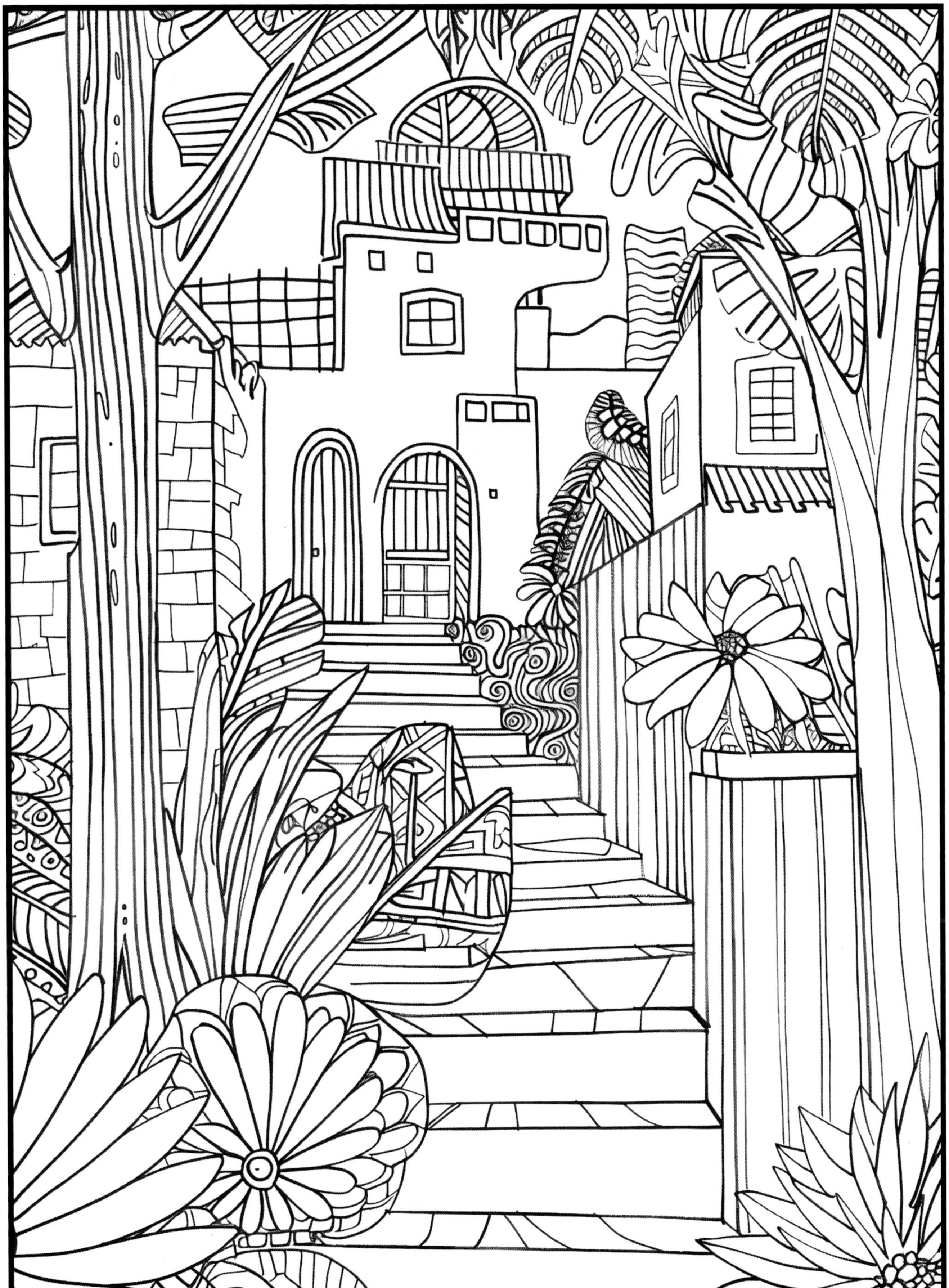

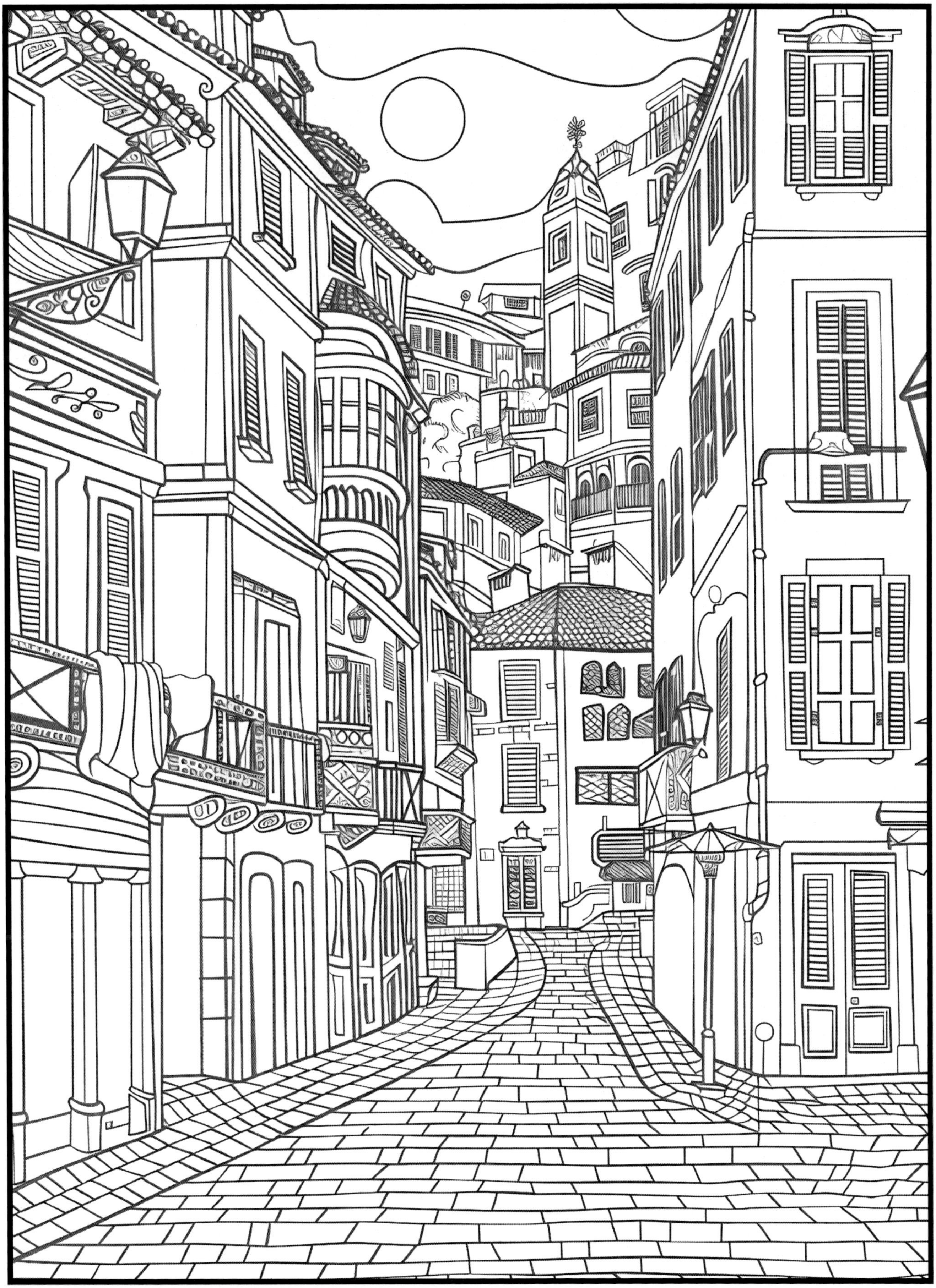

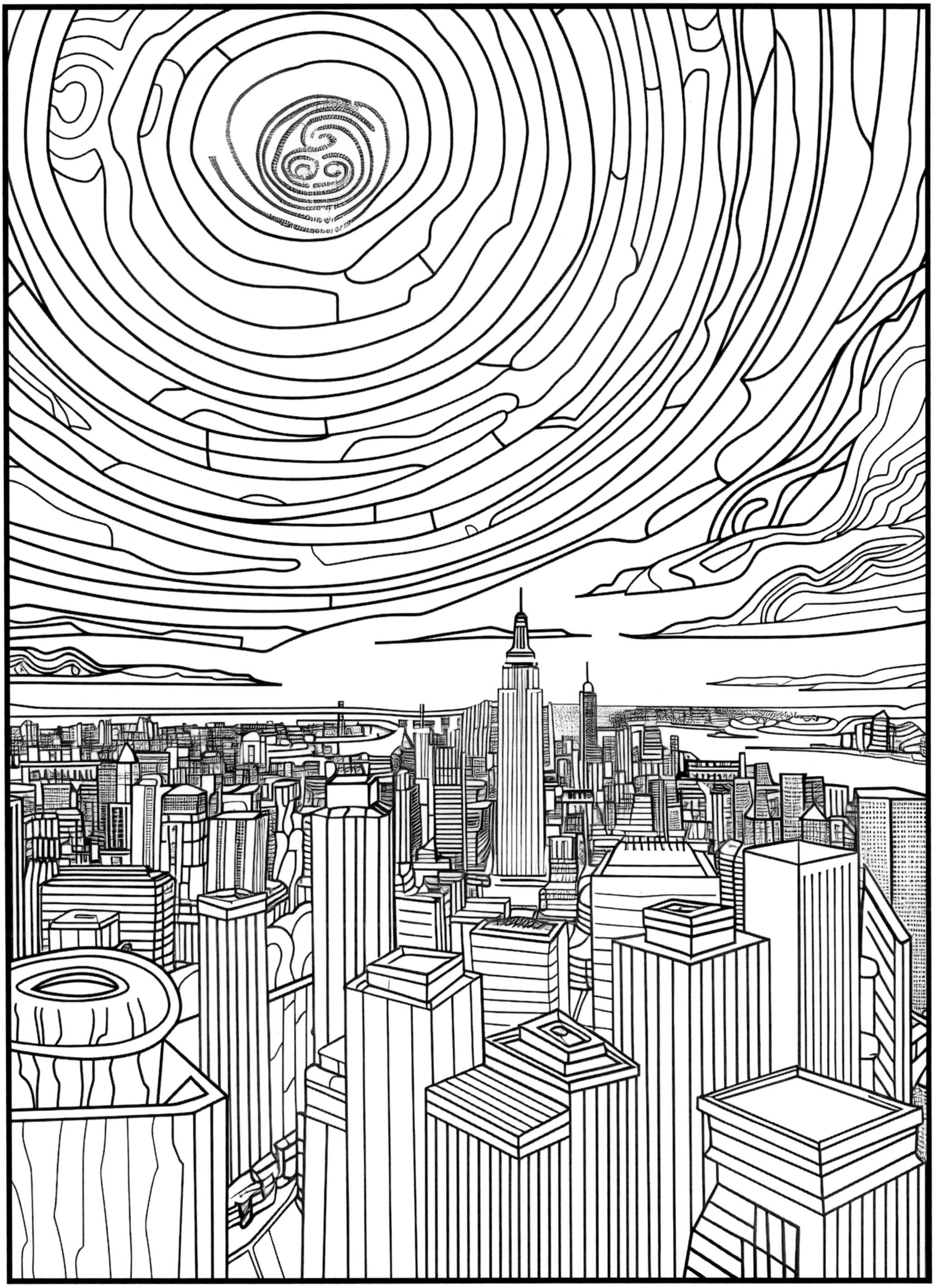

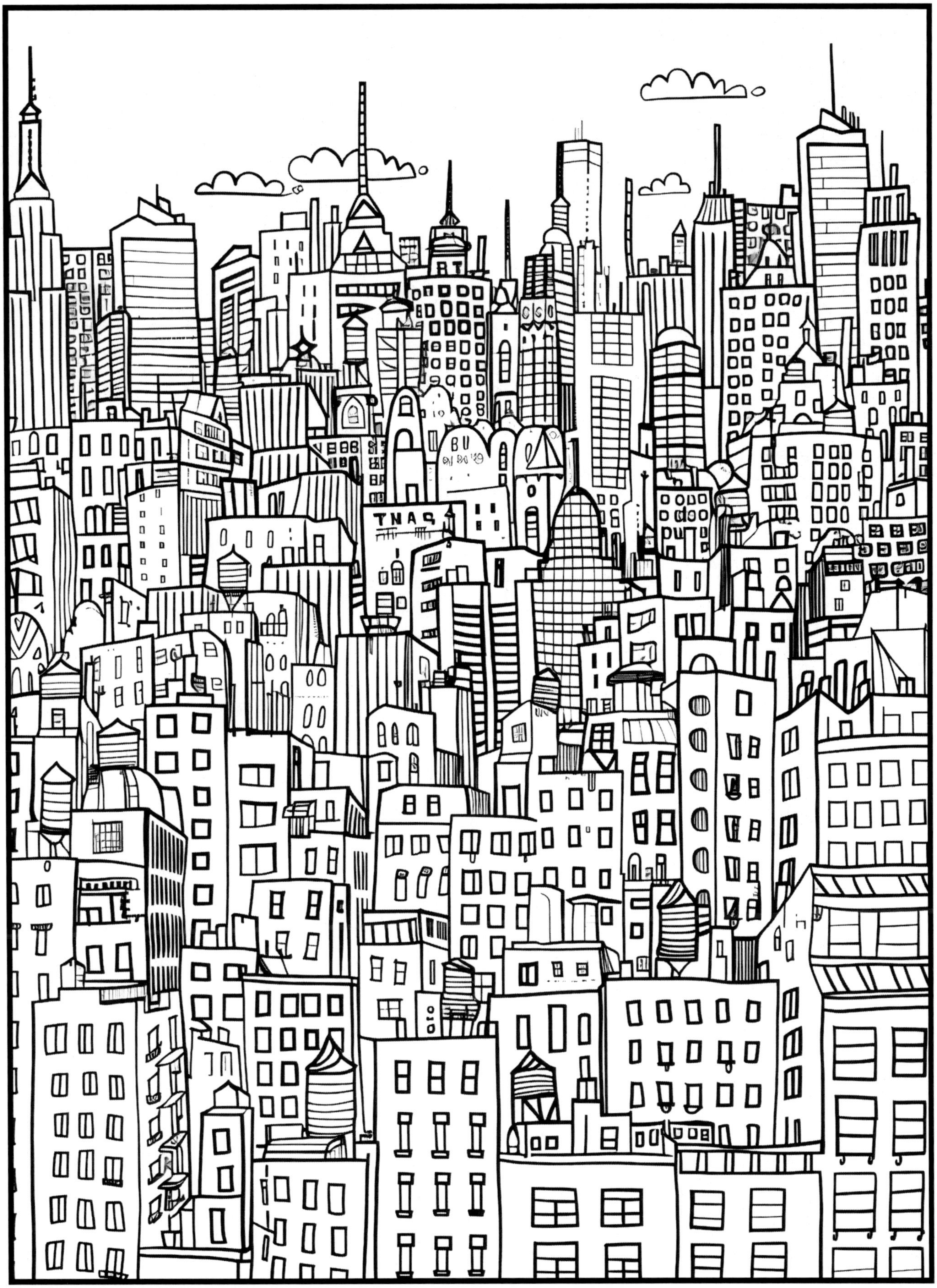

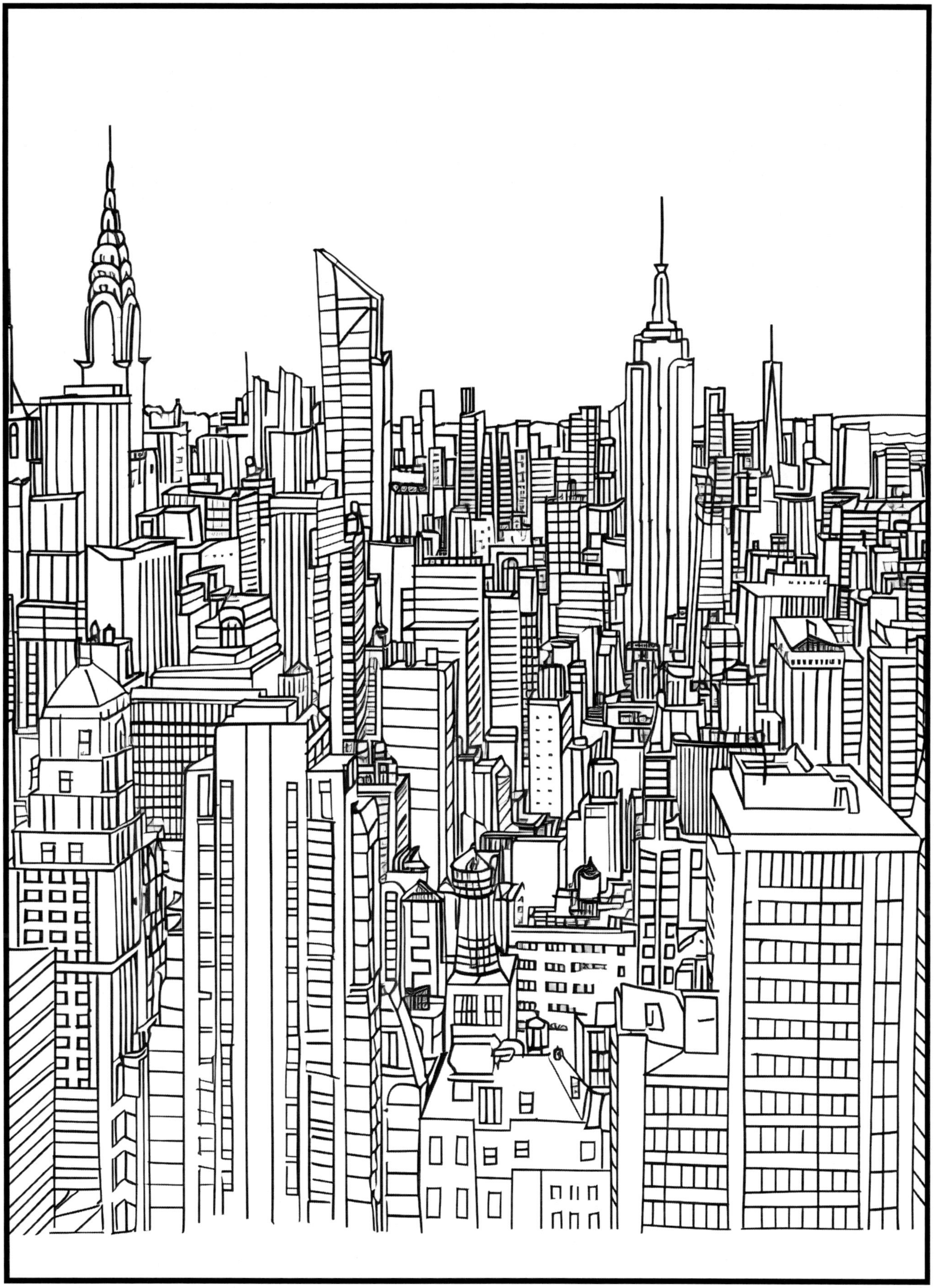

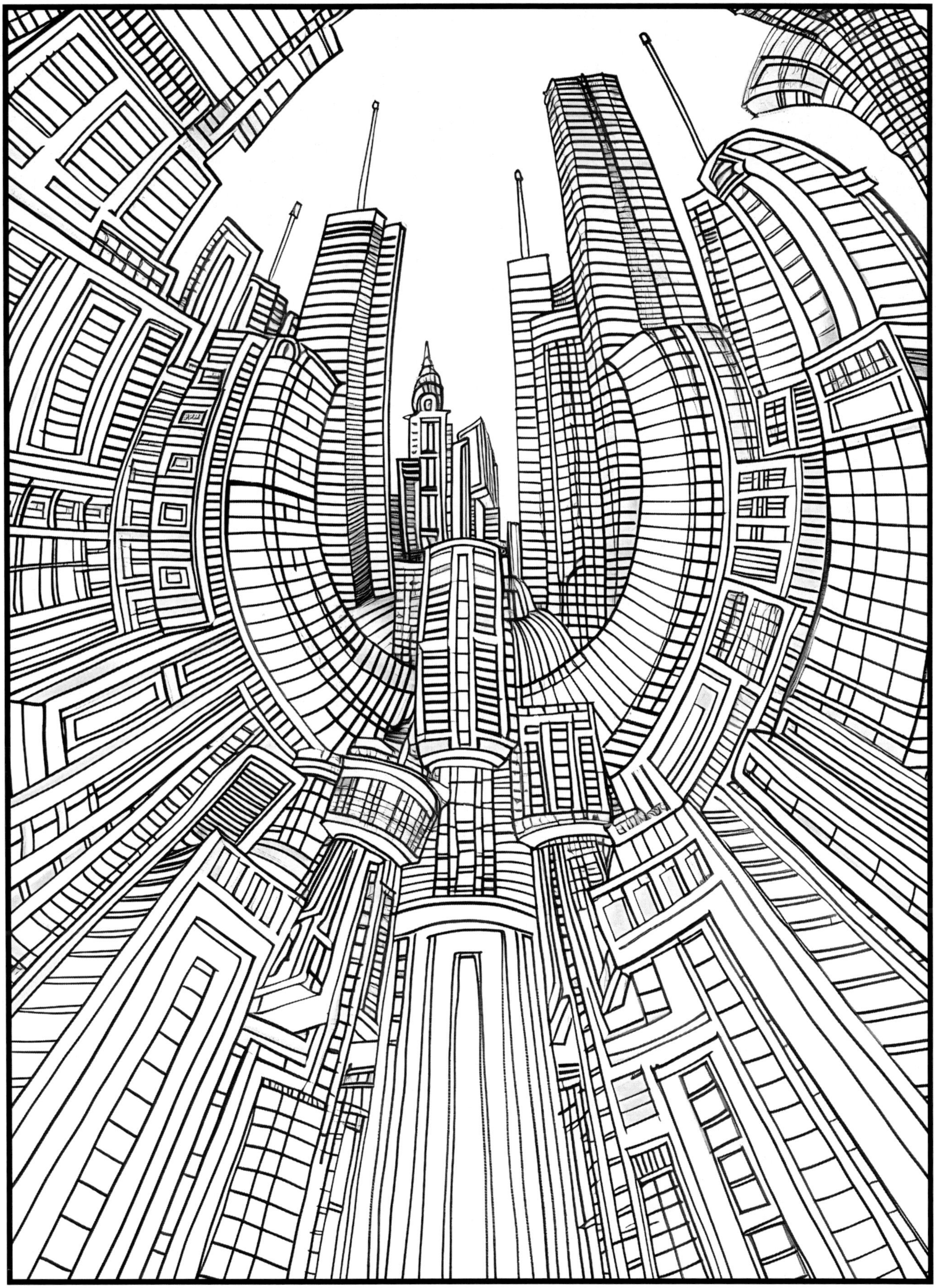

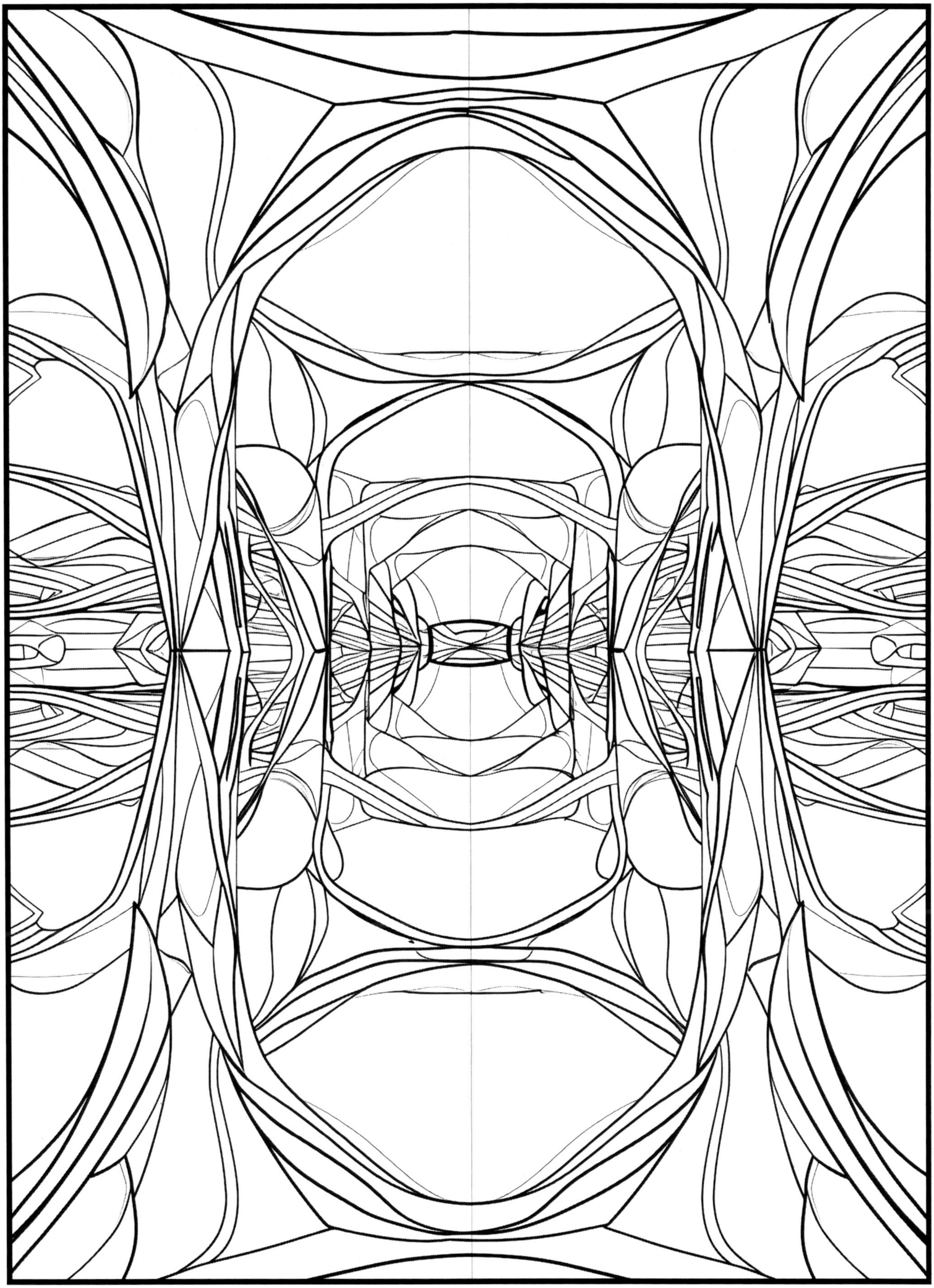

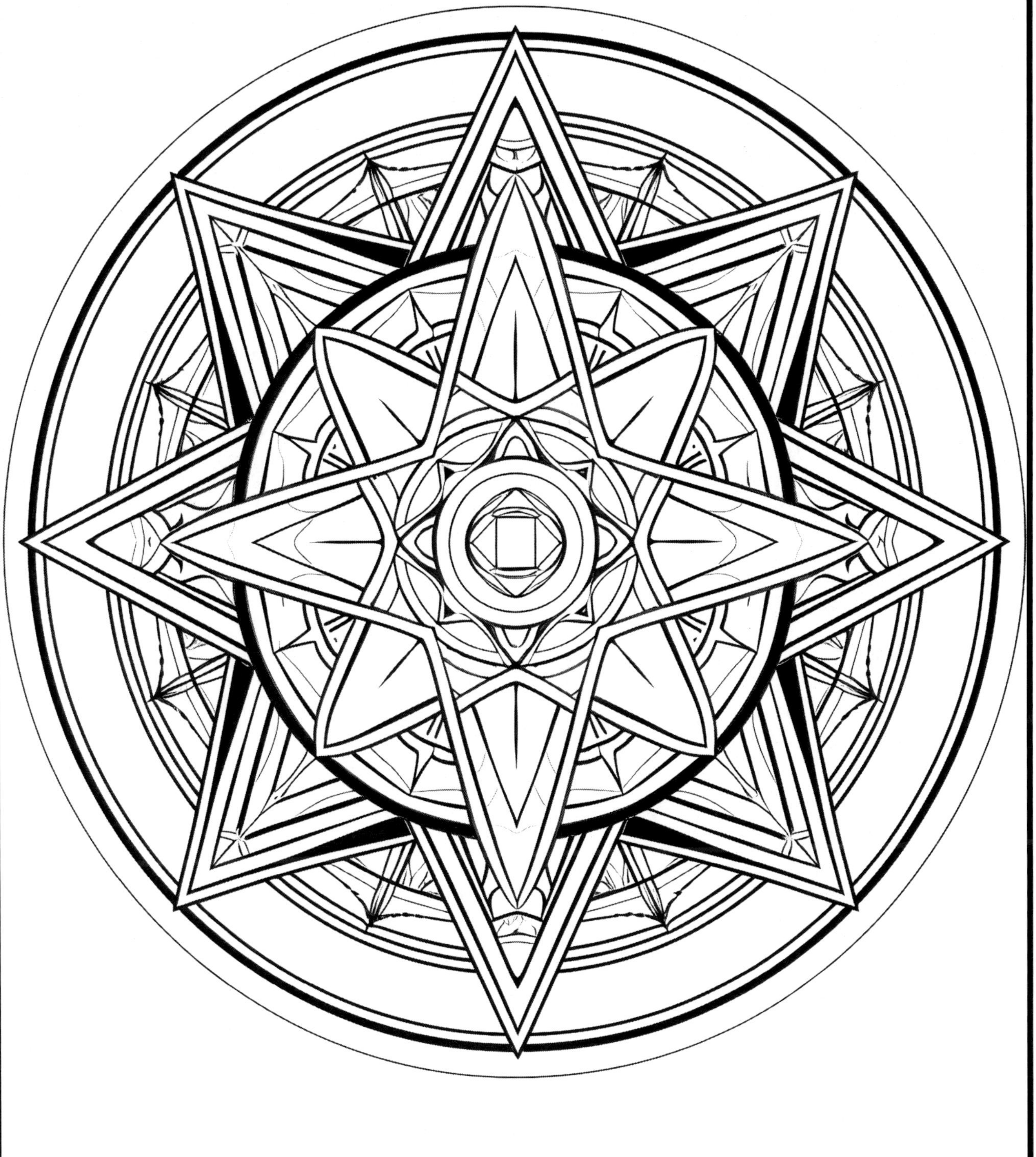

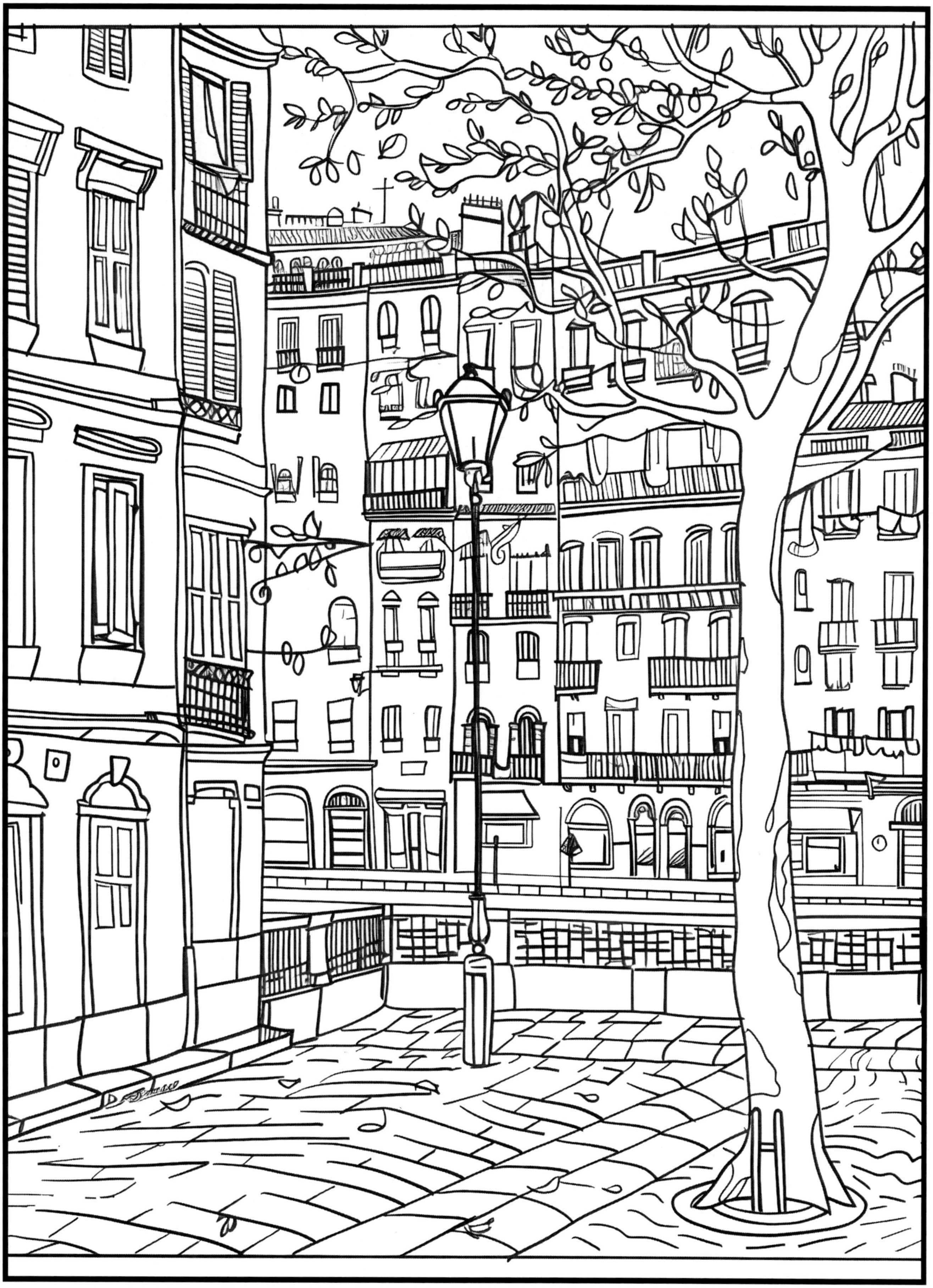

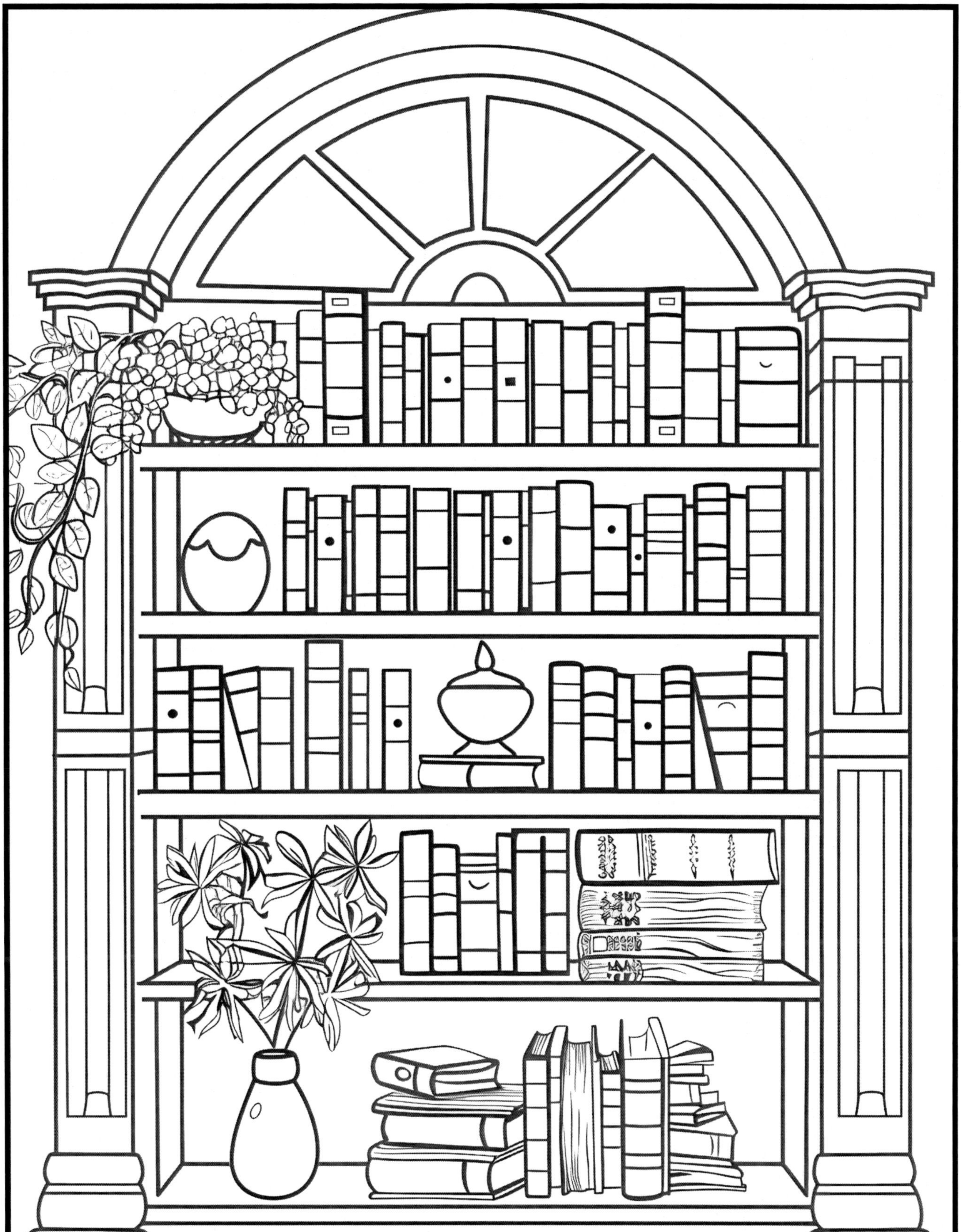

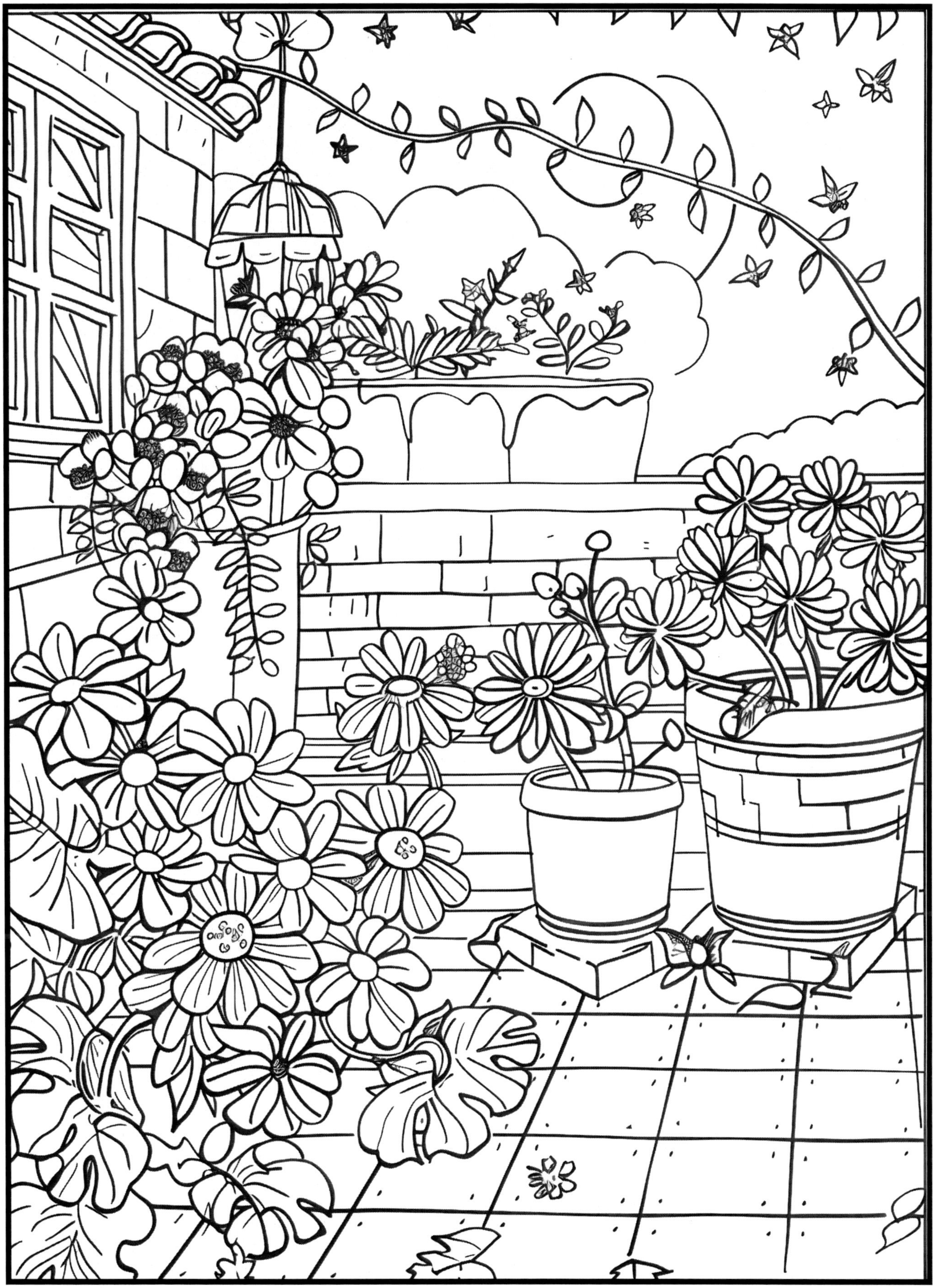

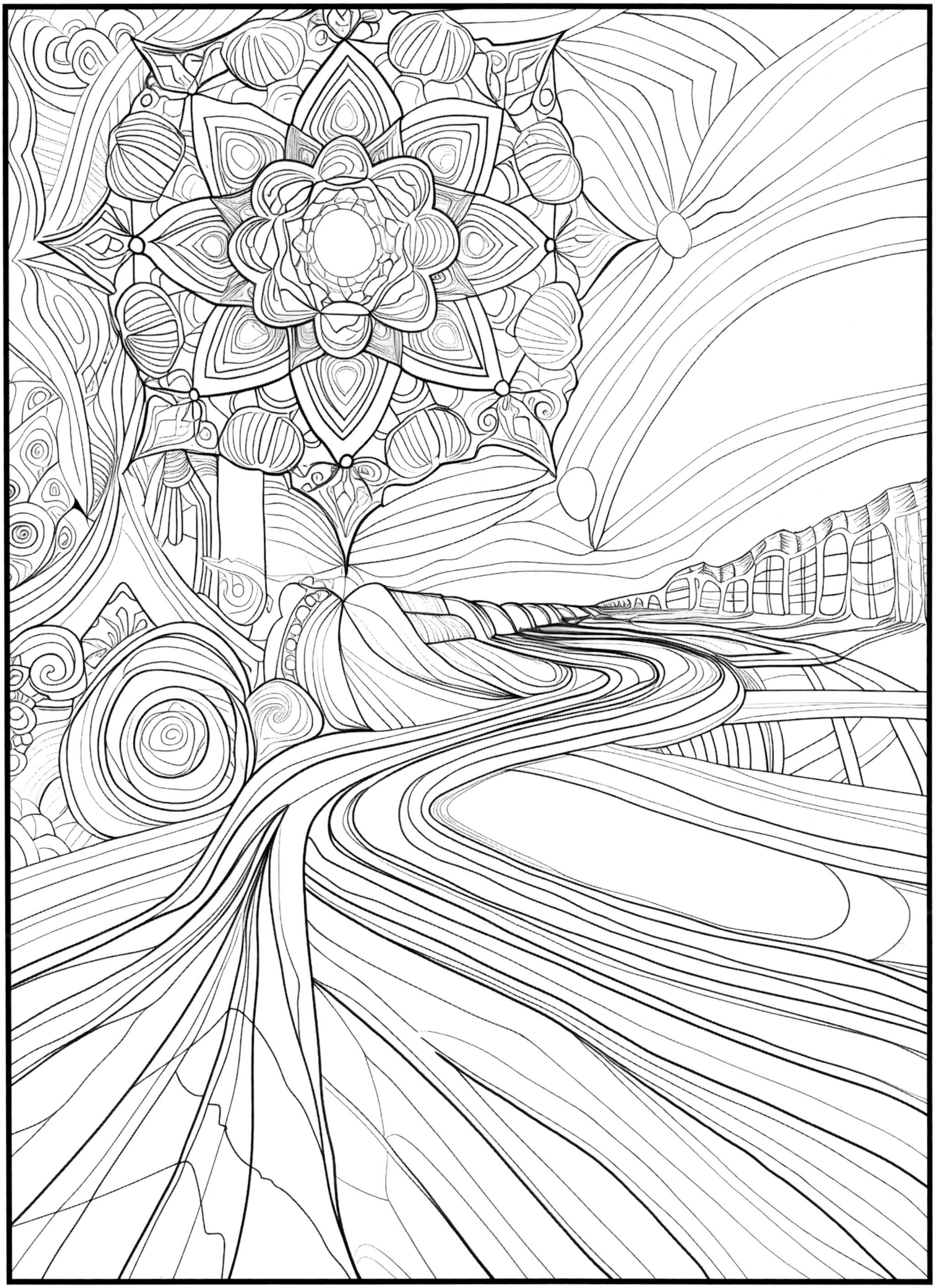

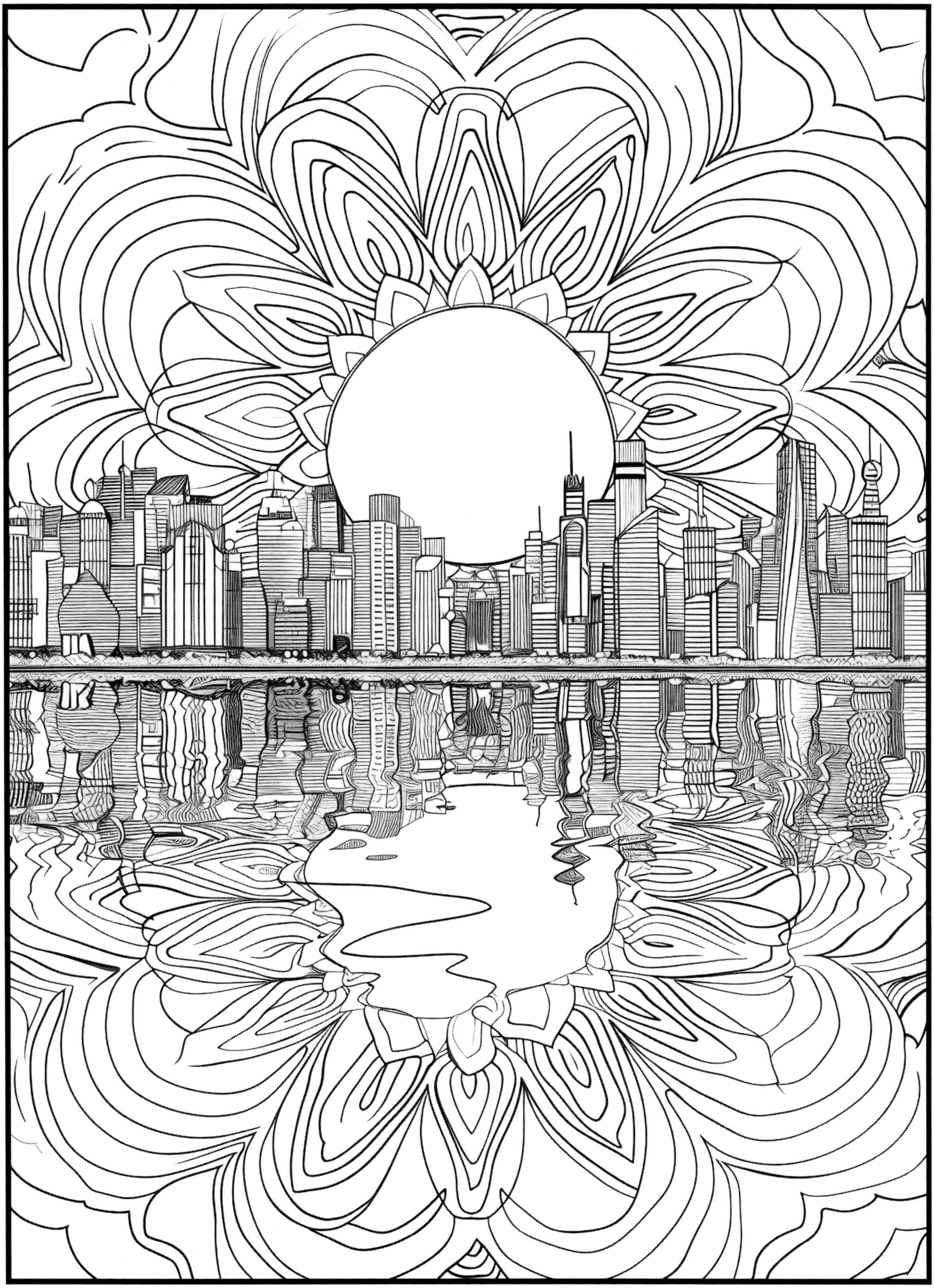

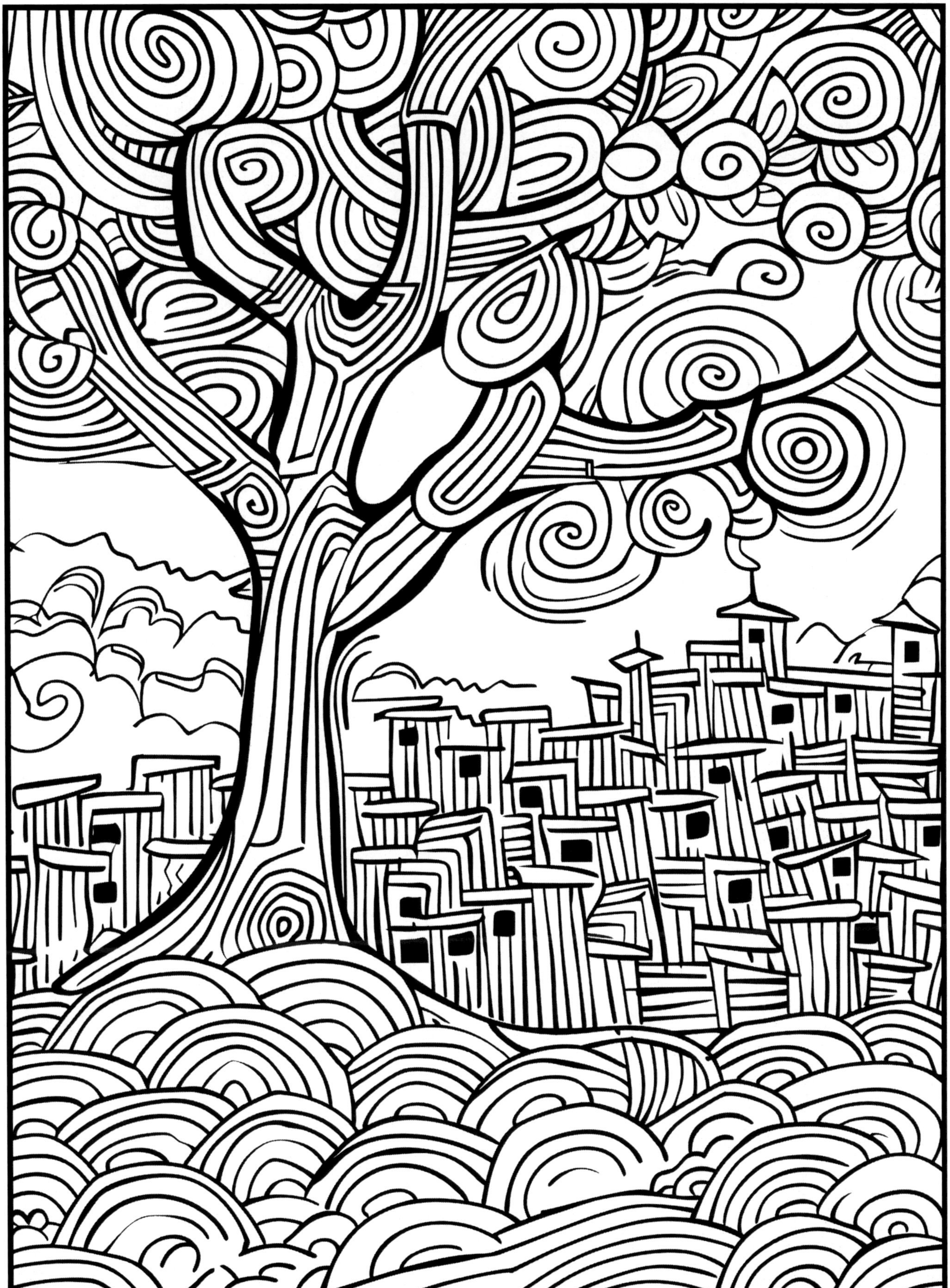

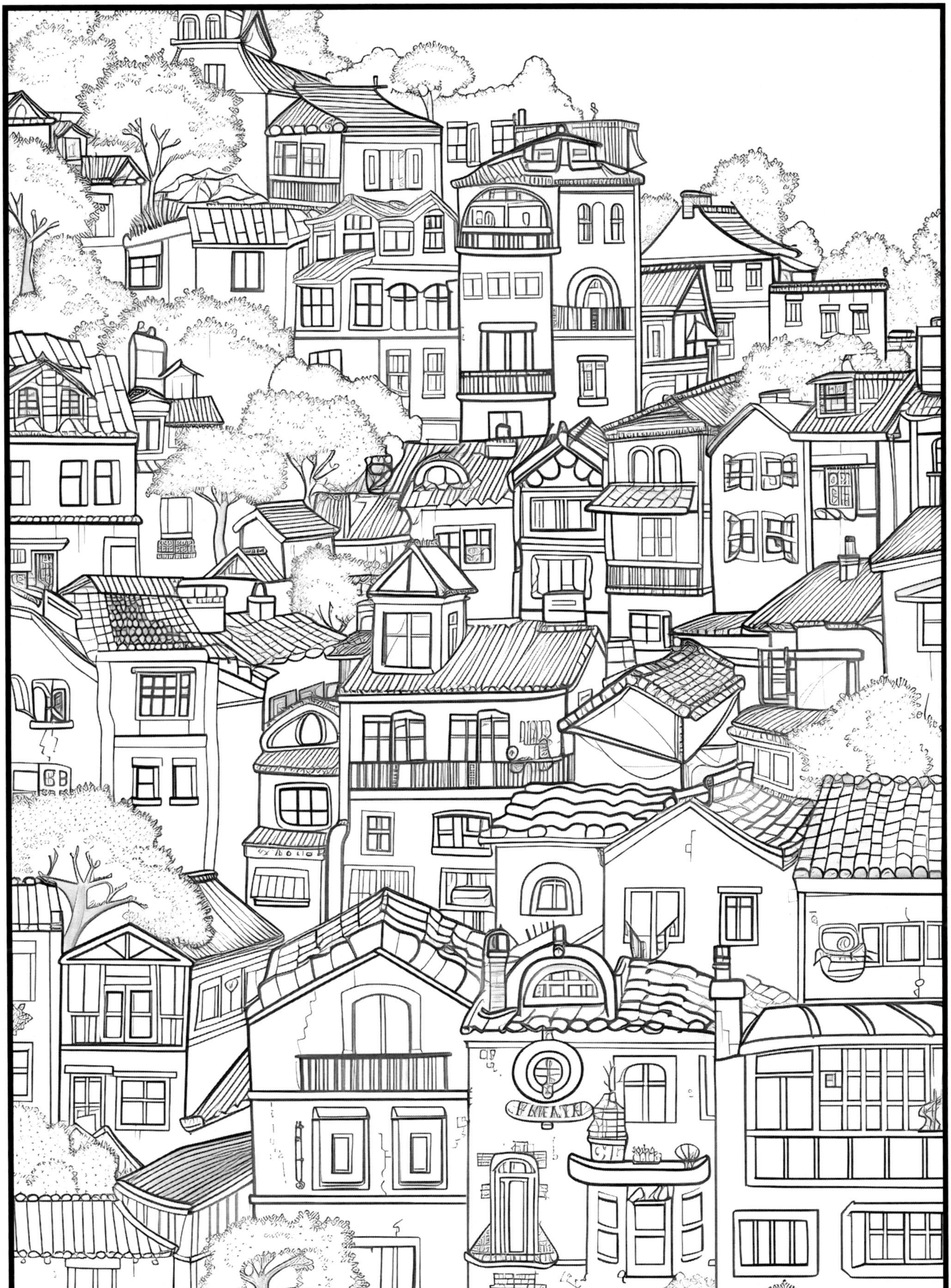

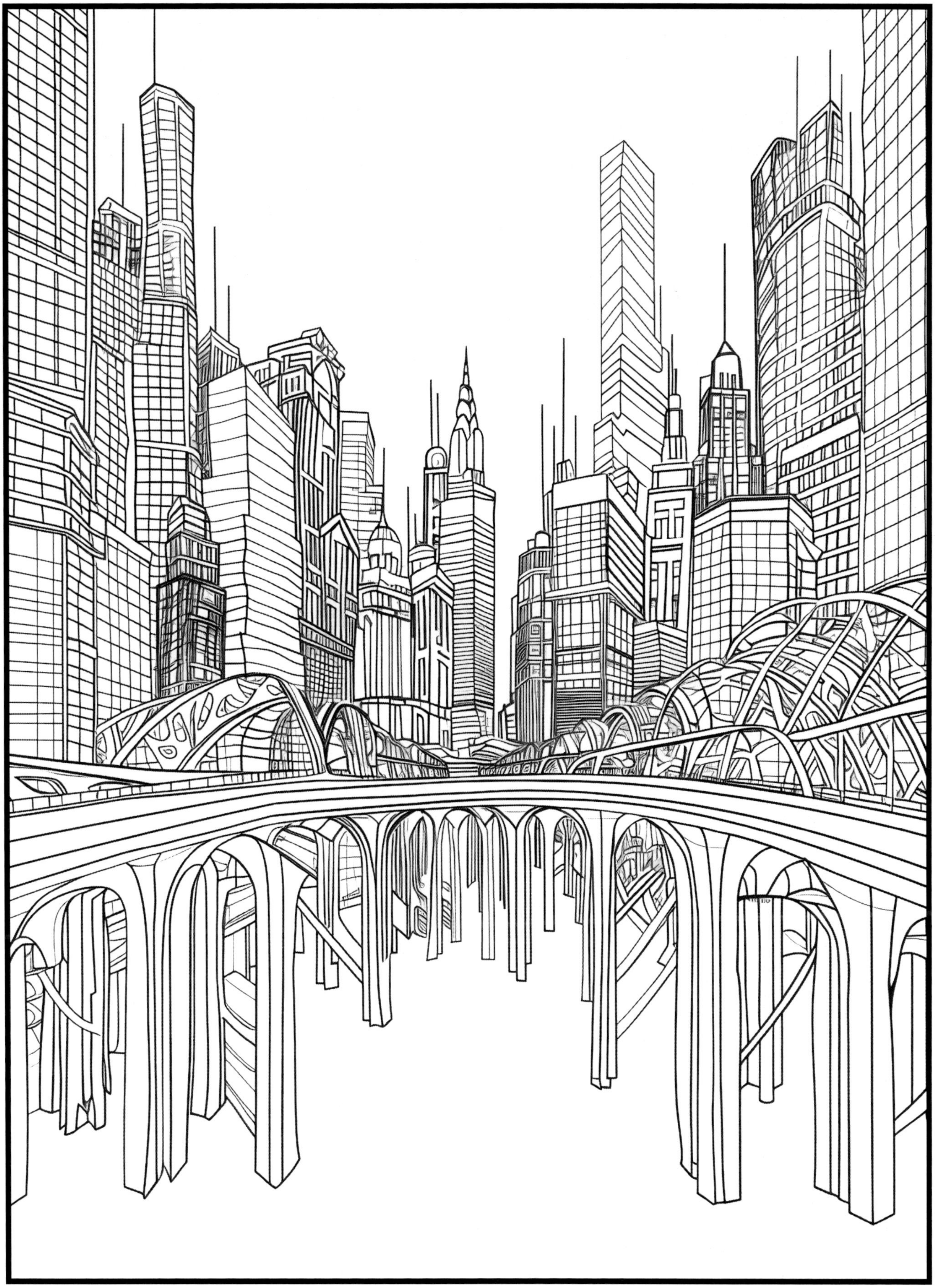

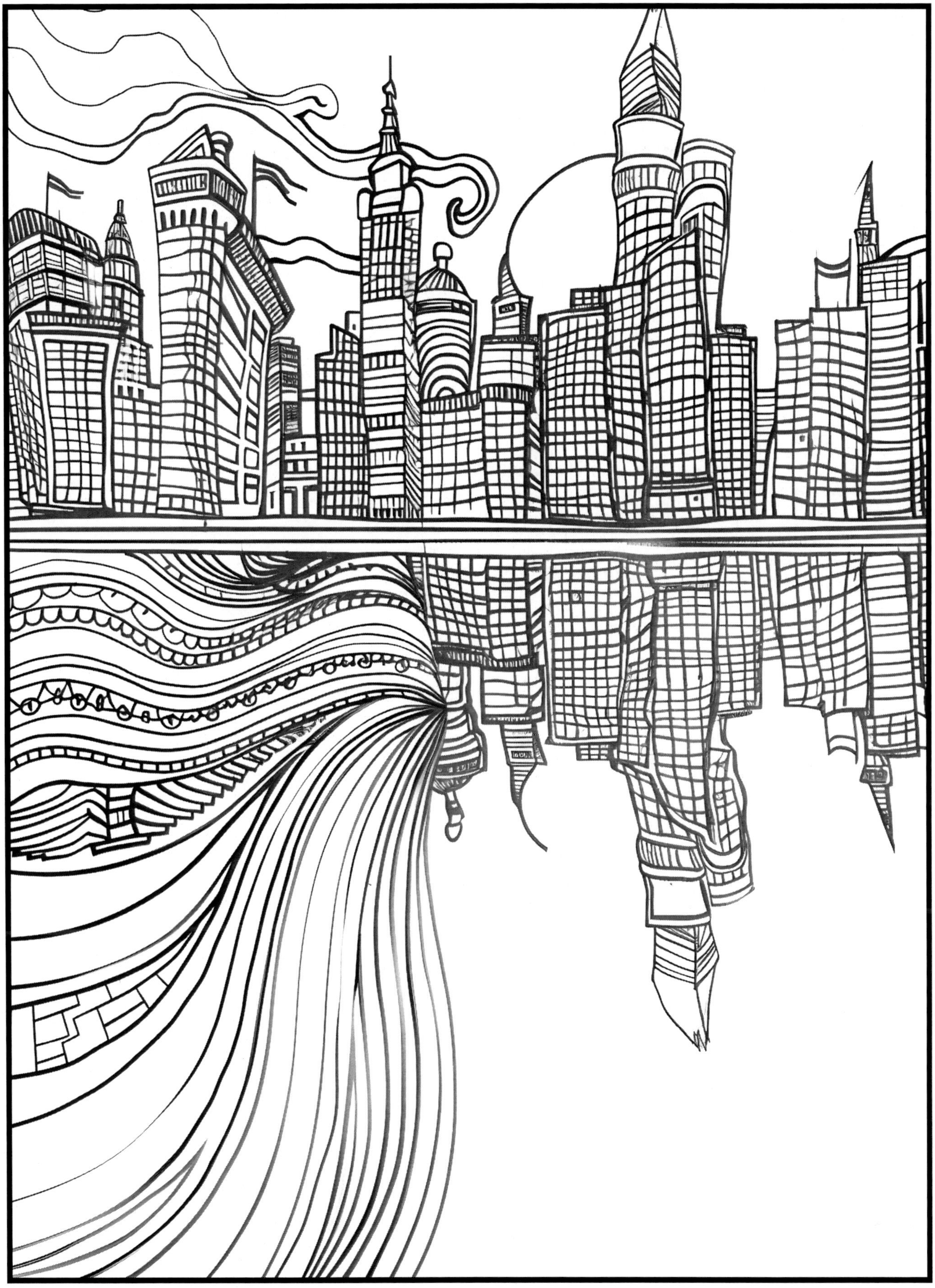

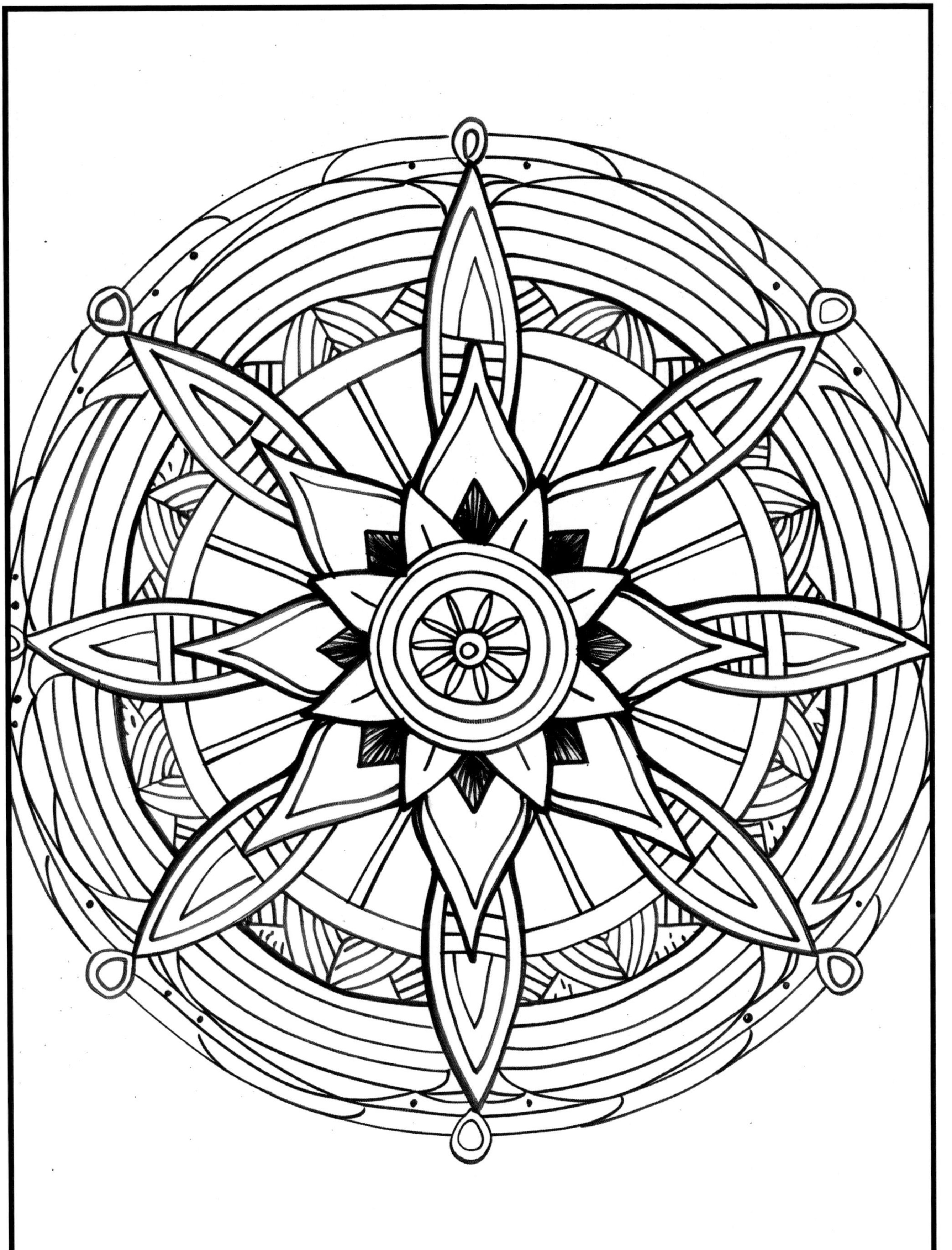

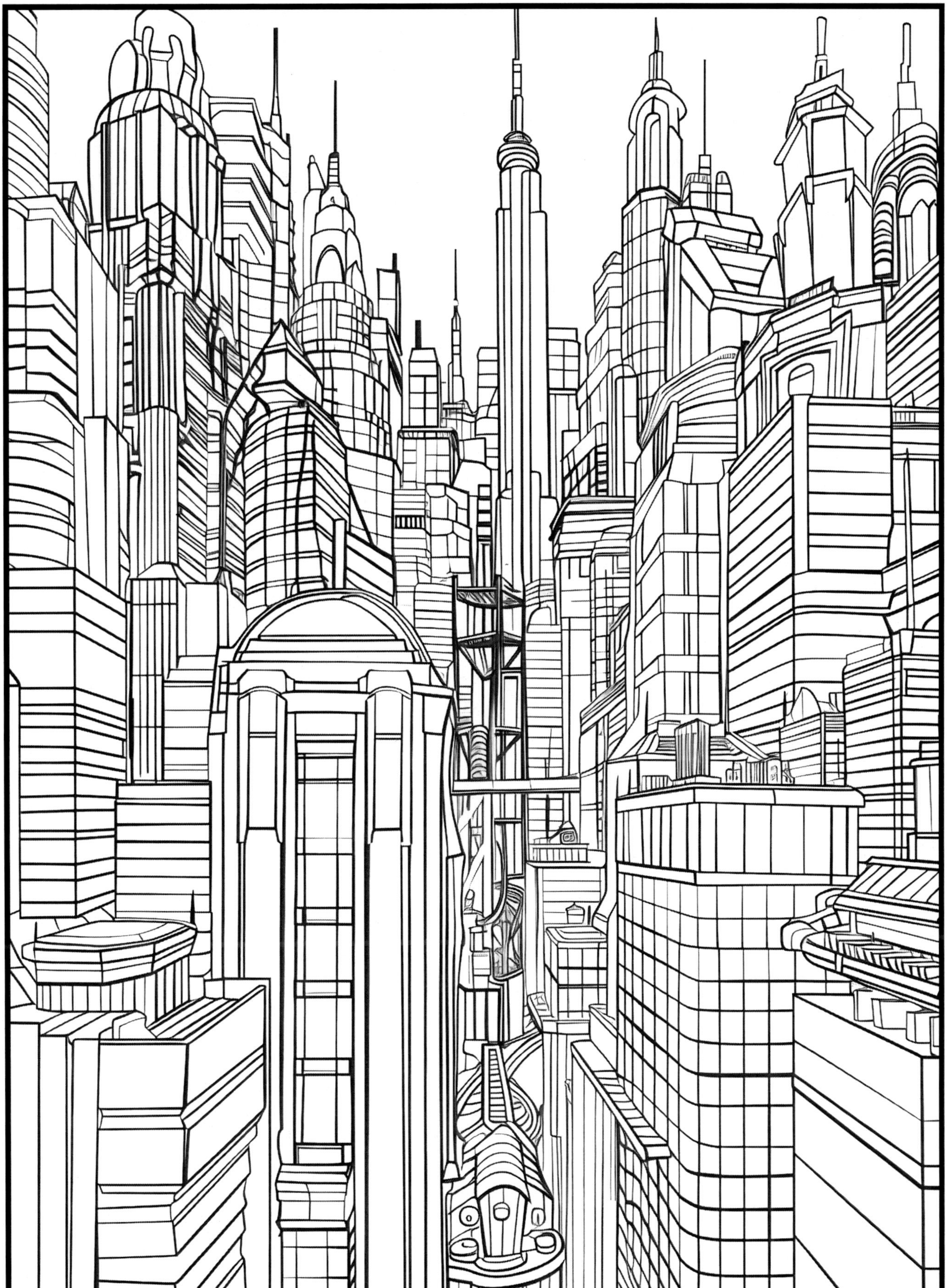

Manufactured by Amazon.ca
Acheson, AB

13562658R00059